the Idler

ISSUE 41 | SUMMER 2008

1 2 5 7 9 10 8 6 4 2

Published in 2008 by Ebury Press, an imprint of Ebury Publishing

A Random House Group Company

The Random House Group Limited Reg. No. 954009

Addresses for companies within the Random House Group can be found at
www.randomhouse.co.uk

A CIP catalogue record for this book is available from the British Library

The Random House Group Limited makes every effort to ensure that
the papers used in our books are made from trees that have been
legally sourced from well-managed and credibly certified
forests. Our paper procurement policy can be
found on www.randomhouse.co.uk

Cover design by the very late William Morris

Typeset by Christian Brett

Printed and bound by Firmengruppe APPL,
aprinta druck, Wemding, Germany

ISBN 978-0-09-192301-3

The views expressed by the contributors do not necessarily reflect those of the editors

Where copyright material has been used we have attempted to trace copyright holders,
any omissions can be rectified in future issues

Editor Tom Hodgkinson
Guest Editors John Lloyd & John Mitchinson
Deputy Editor Dan Kieran *Creative Director Emeritus* Gavin Pretor-Pinney
Editor at Large Matthew De Abaitua *Literary Editor* Tony White
Sports Editor John Moore

To buy books by your favourite authors and register for offers visit www.rbooks.co.uk

WHAT IS THE IDLER

The Idler is a magazine that celebrates freedom,
fun and the fine art of doing nothing.

We want to comfort and inspire you
with philosophy, satire and reflection, as well as
giving practical information to help
in the quest for the idle life.

At

INCLINE PRESS

we make books that are worth keeping.

They are hand made using archival quality materials, printed with metal type and 19th-century machinery. We only work on books that interest us personally, and we have broad interests, especially around 20th-century arts, crafts, and popular culture.

Each book we publish is a deliberately designed craft object, as thoughfully made as a hand-turned bowl or a hand-woven rug. Just as a weaver must choose yarns, colourways, and pattern before beginning to weave, so we select the typefaces, the illustrations, the cloth and paper for book and binding, all of which is intended to complement the text that has first engaged us. And so, by virtue of its bibliosity, each book becomes more than the simple sum of its parts — with all the work done by hand, publishing for us is a process rather than an event. Complex books take time to complete, and we usually publish four or five books each year. Every book gets a printed prospectus, and we put details on our web site.

If you would like your address to be put on
the mailing list, please contact us.

Graham Moss & Kathy Whalen   INCLINE PRESS
36 Bow Street, Oldham OL1 1SJ, Lancs., England
Phone 0161 627 1966   www.inclinepress.com
books.inclinepress@virgin.net

the Idler

CONTENTS

ISSUE 41 ❖ THE QUITE INTERESTING ISSUE ❖ SUMMER 2008

CONVERSATIONS

QI QUESTIONS

ESSAYS

STORIES

IDLE PURSUITS

EDITOR'S LETTER

THIS ISSUE OF THE IDLER HAS BEEN GUEST EDITED BY those two polite revolutionaries, the men from QI, John Lloyd and John Mitchinson. In between running a TV show and writing best-selling books, the pair have found time to put together a set of articles for this mag. It's our collective intention that these pieces express the more radical edge of the whole QI approach to life and the universe. Our natural inborn curiosity and desire to learn, the QI men believe, are ill-served by school and indulged too little in our increasingly frantic adult lives. Philosophizing, a study of history and the natural world, humour and a certain wide-eyed pleasure in the world and its doings: these are the QI antidotes to State-sponsored boredom and the reduction by big business of human beings to commodities and wage slaves.

In the pages that follow, you'll find leisurely conversation the two Johns defending learning for learning's sake. John Mitchinson writes on the warm-hearted genius of William Morris. QI associates Justin Pollard and Elizabeth Garner stand up for subjectivity in history and the importance of nature unenclosed. The QI curriculum proposes ideas for play-based edu-cation, and we present a smattering of QI questions not seen before in the UK. John Lloyd presents his *Notes For A Book I Cannot Be Bothered to Write*.

In the rest of the mag, David Boyle of the New Economics Foundation writes on the fairy renaissance. We print new work from Bronwen Jones and Alice Smith. At the back we suggest ideas on how to live dangerously and die well, as well as how to start your own school and build a bill-free house. There's an interview with Mark Eitzel of American Music Club, and, for your further edification, a reading list chosen by QI.

For a closing thought, I will leave you with the great Robert Louis Stevenson: "My idea of man's chief end was to enrich the world with things of beauty, and have a fairly good time myself while doing so."

Tom Hodgkinson

THE QI MANIFESTO

*Ten steps to making your
life more interesting.*

1. Everything is interesting

You just have to look at it the right way. At the beginning of QI, we set ourselves
the Quite Boring challenge, to se if we could turn up anything that was intrinsically
dull. We failed. Allow yourselves the luxury of looking closely and patiently at anything — a turnip, the history of Chelmsford, a letter from an insurance company —
and new layers of detail come into focus.

2. Ask more questions

QI is one long string of questions. Six year-olds are full of questions, before school
and busy parents teach them that you get on quicker by pretending to know things.
Socrates asked lots of difficult questions. He might have ended up dead (who does-
n't) but he was never bored and he never bored anyone else.

3. We all know less than we think we know

That's what "general ignorance" means. Cultivate humility and a sense of mystery.
"The wise man knows that he knows nothing" (Socrates, again). Despite what some
scientific fundamentalist tell us, we still don't know how or why the universe began,
what consciousness or light are, or even the best way to bring up our children.

4. Look for new connections

We always tell our researchers to only write down things they don't already know.
They find this hard, because formal education is all about recycling and repeating
other people's knowledge (some wag once defined education as the process by
which the notes of the professor appear in the notebooks of the student, without
passing through the mind of either). Interestingness is a lot like humour — it can't
be defined or taught, it's a spark which arcs between two previously unconnected
things.

5. If it's worth writing down, it's worth writing down clearly

Technical terms, jargon and mumbo jumbo might give you the fleeting warmth of belonging to an exclusive club, but they are the enemies of truth. As the anthropologist Margaret Mead once wrote, if you can't explain yourself to a twelve-year-old child, stay inside the university or lab until you have a better grasp of your subject matter.

6. What you leave out is as important as what you leave in

Too many of our knowledge institutions base their authority on spurious claims of "comprehensiveness". We prefer storytellers to panels of faceless academics.

7. Digressions are the point

QI isn't about lists of trivial facts, as we've said, it's about making connections. We're burrowers not grazers. What might start out as a question from the back seat of the car: why do pigeons not fly away sooner might lead to an investigation into how the brain processes visual information; the truth about carrots and night vision; the history of pigeons as a communication device; the Dickin Medal for Animal Bravery; how migratory animals navigate; the chemical constitution of bird dung; the design and ornamentation of medieval dovecotes ...

8. Take your time

The interesting stuff doesn't just roll over and ask to have its tummy tickled. We reckon it takes three hours of reading, thinking and researching to get into the QI zone, when you might notice the unseen link, the mind-altering fact, the life-changing insight, lurking in the fireplace.

9. Walk towards the sound of gunfire

Fear is what stops us, everywhere in our lives, particularly the pointless fear of what other people will think. We know when something isn't right. We should trust our instincts and risk saying so. It's surprising how often things turn out for the best, when you do.

10. You already have everything you need

The most interesting thing you have is you: your instincts, your curiosity, and your own ignorance. But the great paradox is that, in order to be most yourself, you have to shut up about how much you know. The great American philosopher, Ralph Waldo Emerson, wrote that the greatest poets carry "us to such a lofty strain of intelligent activity, as to suggest a wealth which beggars his own". We all have this lofty strain; we just have to find our frequency.

THE BOOK OF IDLE PLEASURES

Ed. *Dan Kieran*
and *Tom Hodgkinson*

with fine illustrations by Ged Wells

Published by Ebury Press £9.99 from all good bookstores
from the 1st May, or online at www.idler.co.uk

CONTRIBUTORS

MATTHEW DE ABAITUA's debut novel, *The Red Men*, is published by Snowbooks

DAVID BOYLE works at the New Economics Foundation and is the author of *Blondel's Song* and many other brilliant books. Find out more at www.david-boyle.co.uk

CHRISTIAN BRETT, the Idler's typesetter, runs Bracketpress at www.bracketpress.co.uk

JAMES BRIDLE's work can be inspected at www.shorttermmemoryloss.com

GRAHAM BURNETT is a gardener, writer and inactivist. www.spiralseed.co.uk

WARWICK CAIRNS' book on measuring is out now (MacMillan)

RU CALLENDAR runs the Green Funeral Company

BRIAN DEAN runs the Anxiety Culture website www.anxietyculture.com

TED DEWAN is an award winning illustrator and cartoonist

BILL DRUMMOND's latest doings can be inspected at www.penkiln-burn.com

ELIZABETH GARNER is a script editor and novelist. Her book *Nightdancing* won the 2003 Betty Trask Award

ELIE GODSI was delegated to by Chris Yates to write thisissue's tea column

PAUL HAMILTON's book of Peter Cook stories is published by Snowbooks

SEBASTIAN HORSLEY is a cat in a hat

TONY HUSBAND is a cartoonist working for *Private Eye* and others

BRON JONES aka Eve Libertine is an artist, illustrator, poet and singer ... all her own work

DAN KIERAN's latest book *Three Men In A Float*, written with Ian Vince, is published by John Murray

JOHN LLOYD is the founder of QI, and he previously produced mighty TV shows such as *Blackadder*, *Spitting Image* and *Not The Nine O'Clock News*

PETE LOVEDAY is creator of the *Russell* comics

HOWARD MALE is an artist and writer

MARK MANNING is a writer, artist and musician. See www.zodiacmindwarp.com

JOHN MITCHINSON is QI's Director of Information and previously occupied various high up posts in the publishing world

CHRIS MOSS is the author of *Landscapes of the Imagination: Patagonia* (Signal Books)

KEVIN PARR is an angler and a gentleman

JUSTIN POLLARD is the author of *The Interesting Bits, the History You Might Have Missed*

PENNY RIMBAUD is away.

GWYN VAUGHAN ROBERTS — Gwyn — is a chronicler of the dark side

JOCK SCOT has still not got a job

ALICE SMITH is an artist. www.alice-wonderland.net

KEVIN TELFER is a London-based author, journalist and photographer. www.kevintelfer.com

SCARLETT THOMAS's latest novel is the existential, steam-punk page-turner *The End of Mr Y* (Canongate)

IAN VINCE's new book, *Three Men In A Float*, is out now on John Murray

JOANNA WALSH is an artist and her website is at www.walshworks.org.uk

GED WELLS runs Insane and illustrated *The Book Of Idle Pleasures* (Ebury)

TONY WHITE is the *Idler*'s literary editor and author of *Foxy-T* (Faber and Faber)

ROBERT WRINGHAM is a comedian and writer. See www.wringham.co.uk

If a chap can't compose an epic poem while he is weaving a tapestry, he had better shut up. William Morris

NOTES from the COUCH

IDLER'S DIARY

Despatches from the loafer's world

Smoker's Corner

¶ As the ravages of the government's ill-considered, uncivilized and frankly impolite smoking ban continue to tear through old convivial Britain, it's worth drawing attention to the occasional courageous rebel. Pub landlord Nick Hogan of the Swan in Bolton was recently fined over £10,000 for failing to enforce the smoking ban. He commented: "I still believe that this legislation is draconian and I am sure that the fight against it will go on. This was not just about smoking. It was about people's rights." Hogan had left notes on the pub's tables which read: "The management and staff believe you have the freedom to choose whether or not you wish to smoke. If you choose to smoke, it is entirely your responsibility." The establishment lickspittles at the *Manchester Evening News*, when reporting the story, called the smoking ban a "great social change", asserted that "the law is the law" and clumsily attacked Hogan as "just another rebel with a cause that was already lost".

This Little Piggie Stayed At Home

Meanwhile, the editor of this magazine got himself into hot water with the busybodies following his decision to have his pigs killed at home. This ancient cottage practice — keeping, killing and eating your own pigs — appears to have been made illegal with a new EU rule. Instead, they have to be killed in the abbatoir. In the old days, and still in civilized countries, country people killed their pigs at home because it is more humane and more straightforward than transporting them to the slaughterhouse. One moment the pig is happily snuffling, and the next it is dead. Clearly the extra cost and hassle of taking them to the slaughterhouse will tend to deter people from keeping pigs at home, meaning more reliance on the vast industrialised systems of food production. William Cobbett wrote that a pig in the back yard was the sign of a contented home, and that "a flitch of bacon hanging in the kitchen does far more for domestic harmony than a thousand Methodist tracts and sermons." The meat from a happy, home-fed pig also tastes better than from slaughterhouse animals. It's time to campaign for a restoration of this ancient custom, and we urge readers to take a look at at www.thislittlepiggiestayedathome.com for more information.

Announcement of a Free Festival

Loafers far and wide will travel to the Exmoor coast again this year for the Lynton and Lynmouth Music Festival, 13th to 15th June. Quality bands, local ales and a seaside setting combine to make this festival one of the quirkiest and most charming of the summer. What's more, it's free. The whole thing is organised and run by unpaid volunteers, makes no profit and is done purely for its own sake. Go to www.llama.org.uk for more details.

More Festival Fun

Look out for an *Idler* presence at other festivals this summer including The Secret Garden Party and Shambala. We had a great time at both these festivals last year, with our friends from the Duke of Uke, the Rebel Soul crew and of course Bloodstone, the medievalist, bardic and merry-making posse run by the redoubtable Daniel Herlakin. This year we hope to recreate a medieval garden for debate and relaxation.

Movie Night

Thanks to Reel Indi of Tapeley Park in North Devon, for asking TH to come and give a talk at one of their film nights. Henry and his gang run a programme of underground and alternative movies at Hector Christie's household in North Devon: www.myspace.com/northdevonactiveyouth

Born Free

To Jock Scot, a child is born, Iris Montgomery. Mother and baby doing well. Dad jobless, toothless and occasionally concussed but also doing well.

To Sarah Janes, a child is also born, Indiana Joy Janes. She is really cute. ◉

READERS' LETTERS

Send us your thoughts and reflections and tell us what you're up to.
Our address is: The Idler, PO Box 280, Barnstaple EX31 4WX

SIT DOWN FOR YOUR RIGHTS

Dear Idler

I too have reached the view that the only protest left is the private, even reclusive, life. I was reminded of a song from the 1970s by Neil Innes:

> Lie down and be counted
> Don't take any more
> Lie down and be counted
> What are we standing for?

Of course there is a way to indulge in the public arena whilst remaining reclusive and that is through the use of multiple aliases. This, however, would be a tricky business and, although I recommend it to the brave and politically committed, it is not for me.

Yours

Private J. Fireextinguisher
Dover Barracks DR4 7QH

UNDER THE SPREADING CHEST-NUT TREE

Dear Idler

I've just finished a degree and have found myself usefully unemployed and so far spent the summer cycling around the Western Isles of Scotland, going from one distillery to the next. But now I've just attempted to claim Jobseeker's Allowance unsuccessfully (because my partner works). *How To Be Free* is giving me solace as I sit under a sweet chestnut tree on Jesus Green, Cambridge, watching the world go by as I wait to begin more study in Oxford.

Yours merrily

Paul Ylioja

THE POWER OF "SO WHAT?"

Dear Idler

I am at work in an office, enjoying the end of a self-rewarded two-and-a-half hour lunch break.

I "worked" (sat around daydreaming and eating) for the UK Atomic Energy Authority for the first five years after leaving school. Most people there were very nice, the pressure to achieve was minimal, and the hours easy. I nevertheless spent many hours walking round the beautiful gardens wishing I was a gardener there.

When I discovered I was about to be promoted, with all the extra responsibilities involved, I decided it was time to leave. The timing was perfect. Between two and five years of service you could leave and claim back every penny of one's pension contributions, so I left at four years, eleven months and two weeks and claimed the lot. My boss was horrified. "How will you accumulate your full forty years contribution?" he pleaded. I said I had no idea how life would pan out in the intervening time and would find the money useful now. He was dead six months after that, at about forty years old, so what good his efforts at accumulating payments?

Incidentally, I spent my money on a thoroughly lazy year off before university while having lots of sex.

A propos of university, I ended up owing a great deal of Poll Tax. By the time I graduated, and to save myself from persecution, I arranged to pay the sum off in small monthly instalments. I "forgot" to pay them after about four months, and have never heard a thing about it since. This is precisely what is described in *How To Be Free*.

My wife just telephoned in a somewhat agitated state to say she was being bullied into going onto an "on-call" rota at Forensics, where she works half-time pathologist. She said she thought they might threaten to terminate her employment if she refused. I said, just say, "no". Call their bluff. If they sacked her, so what? And that is what she will do, and a lot happier she sounded when she hung up.

Yours sincerely
Matthew Black
Australia

BLOW THE HOUSE DOWN

Dear Idler
Like many others, I have been sickened by the smoking ban. Now pubs hold no appeal for me. I can't get comfortable if I can't smoke in a pub — I'd rather be at home, or in someone else's house.

So for fag-addicted idlers whose natural habitat was the local, here is a post-ban code of conduct. It's an early stab, and we'd all welcome sensible additions to it.

When you see an empty pub, don't just walk past it. Go inside and gloat, as loudly as you can, involving as many of the bar staff as possible, but take care not to order anything.

Even if they built huge, weatherproof shelters with comfortable, dry seating installed with plasma screens showing the cricket, don't go anywhere near any pubs that had any sort of non-smoking area before the ban came into effect. Such pubs are run by body fascists.

Never, ever eat food in a pub. The one thought that consoled publicans fretting about the loss of their thirsty, cancer stick devouring regulars was that they'd be able to pull in tourists who didn't know any better and make the money lost on beer sales up by shoving expensive food down their gobs.

Make sure you always take your pint outside for a fag with you. If the cops or their ilk make a fuss about drinking on the street, just point out that you really don't fancy being Rohypnoled tonight, and you wouldn't have dreamed of drinking outside before the stupid bloody smoking ban.

If, while you're outside having a fag, someone swipes your table, don't politely ask for it back. Just punch them in the face.

Never go anywhere near any pub which does not offer smokers shelter from the elements. The smoking area must have seating. Why should smokers be made to stand up in the rain?

Don't talk to the non-smokers. If they come outside to socialise with the smokers, ignore them unless they light up.

If you come across an illegal smoking den, don't post its details on the Internet, and only tell those of your mates most fanatically committed to the cause of illegal tobacco inhalation. [And why not start your own Smokeasy? – Ed.]

Don't buy snuff in a pub. It's shite.
Steve Boxer
London

ONLY DISCONNECT

Dear Idler

Have you seen these two bits from Henry Miller?

"To be silent the whole day long, see no newspaper, hear no radio, listen to no gossip, be thoroughly and completely lazy, thoroughly and completely indifferent to the fate of the world is the first medicine a man can give himself," *The Colossus of Narcissi*.

"There was another thing I heartily disbelieved in — work. Work, it seemed to me, even at the threshold of life, is an activity reserved for the dullard. It is the very opposite of creation, which is play, and which just because it has no *raison d'être* other than itself is the supreme motivating power in life … The world would only begin to get something of value from me the moment I stopped being a serious member of society and became — myself," *Sexus*.

Can one stop being a serious member of society if one has yet to start?

Keep up the good work. 🐌
Paul Davies
Winchester

SKIVERS & STRIVERS

Heroes and Villains of the Idle Universe

Skivers

Doctor Clive James

The erudite intellectual James reminds us of a description of Samuel Taylor Coleridge as the last man who had read everything. James' collection of essays, Cultural Amnesia, is a testament to the restless Idler mind, ranging over twentieth century icons from Miles Davis to Walter Benjamin, Borges to Coco Chanel — a life's work collating voracious reading done in the downtime between writing journalism, fiction or shooting TV shows.

Old School Friends

Make things easier by being balder and fatter than you. Even though you are — by any reasonable standard — bald and fat, old school friends generously exceed you in this regard.

Tea Appreciation Society

Tea lovers unite in appreciation of mellow beauty. Go to their website at www.teaappreciationsociety.org and read their rousing manifesto in praise of the noble leaf.

Escapades

Subversive, situationist-inspired zine that explores the idea of "creative interventions" to attack boredom in everyday life. Available from www.activedistribution.org

Credit Crunch

Satisfyingly onomatopoeic end to the long boom, as if King Kong in a pinstripe suit took one bite too many out of an enormous chocolate bar. Finally us Idlers can get some peace from the yabber of the markets and instead enjoy the blissful silence of derivatives experts sailing downward through the crisp blue morning air.

THESE DAYS I
EAT MOSTLY
PIRATED FOOD
OFF THE INTER-
NET.

Strivers

Bourgeois Quick-Buck Schemes

Because the middle classes consider the lottery beneath them, the last few years have seen a boom in easy money plans for the poor souls trapped by onerous mortgages and all-consuming careers. Back in the 1990s, the novel was seen as a financial and spiritual way out of the dolour. Then, after the success of The Weakest Link, the race was on to coin it in with a new TV format. The hordes moved on to dot com start-ups, and when that went belly-up, turned to property development and then Christmas crapbooks. Now that market is saturated, our sources tell us the bourgeoisie have moved onto flogging homemade preserves and even fancier forms of chocolate. Because no way are you going to do that office job forever.

Russell Brand

We love Russell Brand. We even read his Booky Wook, which is one third of a decent book. By our calculation that is one sixth better than the other mental cholesterol clogging up the bestseller list. But Russell is working too hard, stretching himself too thinly, failing to replenish the reservoir of his talent and thus doling out the last shakes of his initial inspiration like an old man with an engorged prostate, doomed to piss forever at the urinal that is television. As the magazine exhorts, Take A Break.

Attention

Attention is survival. Babies have to attract attention from adults to ensure they are fed and protected. Parents willingly give up being the centre of attention to care for their off-spring. Therefore the seekers of attention — brands, political parties, Russell Brand — are our babies. And we have spoilt our off-spring with too much attention. All would thrive from a little more parental indifference. 🐌

Idle Pleasures

SOHO

¶ If you eliminate heroin and crack cocaine, I am amazed to find that almost all my pleasures can be, and mostly are, shared by a dog. ¶ Like a dog, squalor is my natural setting. I live on Meard Street — shit street — which suits me. Soho is a sewer with service from my flat. ¶ I love the dim alleyways of Soho, where no sunlight, not even a hated breath of fresh air ever penetrates. From the glitter to the litter, from the whore to the poor; the harlots and hunted have pleasures of their own to give that the vulgar herd can never understand. For in Soho, every human flaw, from a single wound to the corrupt heart, has been sealed in the amber of artifice. ¶ Soho shows life at ground zero. Where human beings bare their teeth across this jubilant wasteland. It is the naked jaws of hunger; the naked jaws of need. It is nothing but a stomach and a penis. Living in Soho is like coming all the time. ¶ I have no need to go beyond my Soho. The adventure, the great adventure, is to see something unknown appear — surge forth each day in the same place. It is greater than all the trips around the world. Every day in a suit made to measure I go in pursuit of pleasure. 🐚

Sebastian Horsley

GedWells

THE HUMAN BRAIN IS THE MOST COMPLEX OBJECT IN THE KNOWN UNIVERSE. THIS STATEMENT IS LESS IMPRESSIVE WHEN YOU CONSIDER HOW LITTLE OF THE UNIVERSE IS KNOWN TO US. HOWEVER MUCH WE MAY KNOW ABOUT A STAR 100,000,000 LIGHT YEARS AWAY FROM US, WE DON'T HAVE A CLUE ABOUT THE COMPLEXITY OF THE OBJECTS ON ITS PLANETS. STILL, IT'S BETTER THAN NOTHING.

OF COURSE NOT ALL BRAINS ARE OF EQUAL COMPLEXITY. THE ONE SHOWN OPPOSITE, THAT OF A RANDOMLY SELECTED 28 YEAR OLD MALE FROM NORTH DEVON, IS A NICE SIMPLE ONE, IDEAL AS AN EXAMPLE FOR THE BEGINNER IN HUMAN HEAD STUDIES.

KEY ① SITE OF THIRD EYE (DISUSED). ② PHYSICAL ACTIVITY CENTRE (DUE FOR DEMOLITION). ③ LOST OPPORTUNITIES, ABANDONED IDEALS, ETC. ④ ARCHIVE, MAINLY DEVOTED TO FOOTBALL, CARS, TELEVISION REALITY SHOWS AND OLD JOKES ⑤ THE OLD SITE OF THE 'GOD SPOT', DEMOLISHED TO MAKE WAY FOR EXPANSION OF ④ AND ⑥ ⑥ LIBIDO CENTRE AND PORN VIDEO COLLECTION. ⑦ EYE (EVOLVED IN EARLIER SPECIES TO OBTAIN VITAL VISUAL INFORMATION, BUT FORTUITOUSLY SUITABLE FOR VIEWING SPLATTER MOVIES, VIDEO GAMES, PORN SITES, ETC. ⑧ VISUAL DATA SLOT. ⑨ MOTIVATION SELECTOR (APPARENTLY UNCONNECTED TO OTHER SYSTEMS). ⑩ UNDIFFERENTIATED VISUAL IMAGES CONTAINER. ⑪ WASTE PIPE FOR INSTANTLY FORGOTTEN VISUAL INFORMATION. ⑫ VISUAL SELECTION CONTROL. ⑬ SNOT STORAGE.

   IF CONFUSED, TAKE A BREAK, HAVE A COFFEE... OKAY, NOW CONTINUE.—
⑭ NASAL INLET FOR SCENTS AND DRUGS. ⑮ AROMA EXTRACTION CONTROL. ⑯ AROMA WASTE BUCKET. ⑰ ORAL INLET FOR FOOD, ALCOHOL AND DRUGS. ⑱ DISCHARGE PIPE FOR SPEECH, ANIMAL NOISES AND VOMIT. ⑲ INLET PIPE FOR AFOREMENTIONED. (JUNK) FOOD, CHIPS, BOOZE AND DRUGS. ⑳ SPEECH CENTRE. ㉑ VOICEBOX ㉒ POLITICAL CORRECTNESS FILTER (PERMANENTLY DISABLED). ㉓ MAIN REGURGITATION CONDUIT. ㉔ FOOD AND DRUGS SEPARATION UNIT. ㉕ FOOD TUBE. ㉖ AND ㉗ DRUGS AND ALCOHOL ROUTEWAYS. ㉘ BEHAVIOUR MODIFICATION AND DEGREDATION CYLINDER. ㉙ PSYCHEDELIC SUBSTANCE PIPE. ALSO USED AS BYPASS FOR RANDOM PSYCHOTIC VISUAL EVENTS. ㉚ EXCESS DRUG ROUTE. ㉛ EAR MECHANISM. MANY POSSIBLE USES, BUT IN THIS SUBJECT MAINLY EMPLOYED TO HEAR MUSICAL SOUNDS, MOSTLY THROUGH HEADPHONES FROM VARIOUS PIECES OF EQUIPMENT. ALSO HANDY FOR CELLPHONE. OCCASIONALLY EMPLOYED TO DETECT AGGRESSION OR SEXUAL INNUENDO. ㉜ MUSIC TRIAGE UNIT ㉝ WASTE MUSIC PIPE ㉞ CONDUIT FOR SELECTED RAP, HIP-HOP, GARAGE, HARDCORE TECHNO, DEATH METAL AND CLASSIC RUGBY SONGS. ㉟ MIXING TANK, BLENDS MUSIC AND DRUGS ON SEMI-RANDOM BASIS ㊱ SEEPAGE OUTLET, WHICH RELEASES A GENERAL BACKGROUND LEVEL TO MOST PARTS OF THE BRAIN. POSSIBLY IN SOME WAY LINKED TO ⑨. ㊲ AREA DEVOTED TO PRACTISING FOR SENILITY: SHORT TERM MEMORY LOSS, MOBILITY PROBLEMS, LIGHT COMA. ㊳ TERRA INCOGNITA, HOME OF DISCARDED EXPERIENCES AND IRRETRIEVABLY LOST DATA. ㊴ OVERSPILL ROOM FOR CAREFULLY SUPRESSED AND PAINFULLY EMBARRASSING MEMORIES.

IF DEEPLY BORED OR JUST TOO THICK TO UNDERSTAND THIS QUANTITY OF TECHNICAL INFORMATION, THIS IS PROBABLY A GOOD PLACE TO STOP...

㊵ PSYCHEDELIC EXPERIENCE CENTRE. ㊶ SUPERCHARGER PIPE, CONVEYING MUSIC/OTHER DRUGS MIXTURE TO ㊵. ㊷ MONITOR SCREEN. SEEMS TO HAVE A VITAL PARANOIA INDUCING FUNCTION WHICH SERVES TO EXERCISE THE MIND, KEEPING INTELLECTUAL FUNCTIONS TICKING OVER WITH CONSPIRACY THEORY INVESTIGATION, INTRODUCES CAUTION RE. DRIVING, THE POLICE AND LARGE MEAN MALES. ㊸ FOOD-TO-VOMIT SHORT CIRCUIT VALVE OPERATIVE. ㊹ ERECTILE FUNCTION WINCH OPERATIVE. ㊺ EXCRETARY SYSTEM COMMAND POST. PROXIMITY TO ㊵ SIGNIFICANT.

A CHILD'S GUIDE TO THE HUMAN HEAD

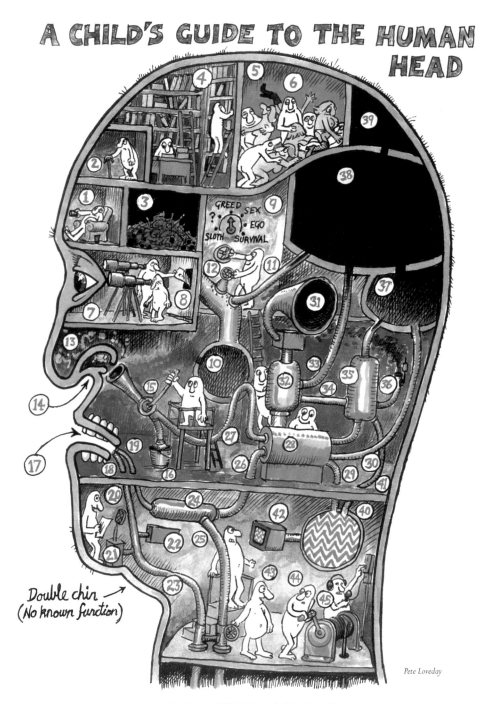

Double chin
(No known function)

Pete Loveday

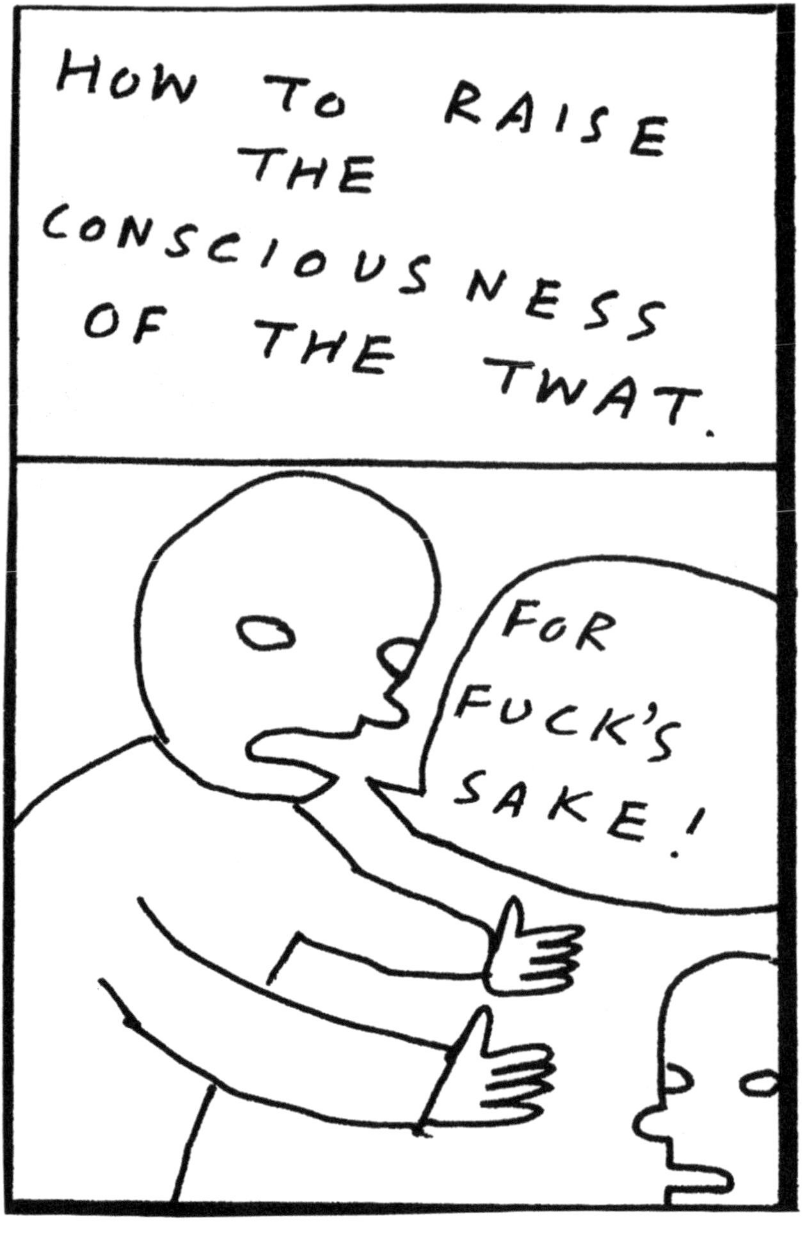
HOW TO RAISE THE CONSCIOUSNESS OF THE TWAT.
FOR FUCK'S SAKE!

THE TRUTH ABOUT TIME

Brian Dean of *Anxiety Culture* says time management systems and scheduling destroy the spirit and don't work anyway

SCHEDULING: A WASTE OF TIME?

¶ In the 1820s, when George Stephenson's Liverpool-to-Manchester railway went behind schedule and over budget by 45%, everyone involved could be excused, as the discipline known as project management hadn't yet been invented. In the intervening 180 years, managing projects has become an industry in its own right — but time and cost overruns are still the norm:

- A 2006 National Audit Office review of 20 large UK defence projects found a total delay of 36 years — an average of one year, nine months per project.

- An international study on the management of public projects, published in 2002, found that almost nine out of ten projects went over budget, with overruns of 50–100% common.

- 71% of IT projects go behind schedule, over budget and / or under scope, according to a 2004 industry study by the Standish Group.

- 75% of UK government building projects are completed late and over budget, according to a 2001 BBC report.

[*Sources: National Audit Office's 'Ministry of Defence: Major Projects Report 2006', 24/11/2006;'Underestimating Costs in Public Works', Journal of the American Planning Association,Vol. 68, No. 3, Summer 2002;'CHAOS Report 2004',The Standish Group; BBC Radio 4 'Today', 11/1/2001*]

UNDERESTIMATING BY BILLIONS

¶ The public ends up paying billions for projects which are either cancelled or which would never have received the go-ahead if the true cost had been known from the start:

- An ID card scheme for benefit claimants was scrapped in 1999 after nearly £1bn was spent on it. The National Audit Office found that "skimping" at the start of the project led to "vast delay and waste of money". It added: "Mistakes of this kind are made time and time again".

- The National Programme for IT (an NHS project) was originally expected to cost £2.3bn over three years, but in June 2006 the total cost was estimated by the National Audit Office to be £12.4bn.

- The cost of the Jubilee Line (London underground railway) was estimated in 1994 at £2.1bn. The final cost (it was two years late) was £3.5bn.

- The Eurofighter jet (a UK/European project) cost, in total, £50bn. It was £30bn over budget and completed a decade late, according to a 2003 BBC2 report.

- A £1bn upgrade to the Tornado GR-4 fighter jet left it unable to fire modern "smart" bombs, giving it less capability than before the "upgrade". As a result, the jets couldn't be used in the Kosovo conflict, forcing British forces to rely on older GR-1s and Harrier jets.

- The New Deal welfare-to-work scheme was originally budgeted at over £5bn, with an estimated cost of £4,000 for each job. In July 2000 an independent report put the real cost at £11,000 per job.

- Refurbishment and building work on the headquarters of MI5 and MI6 cost over half a billion pounds — more than twice the estimate.

- The Channel Tunnel was financed with private money, but this didn't stop it going over-budget by £5.2bn (original estimated cost: £4.8bn; final cost: £10bn).

[Sources: BBC News Online, 5/9/2000; Wikipedia (NHS cost); The Guardian, 7/3/2000; 'Eurofighter', BBC2, 11/11/03; The Guardian, 7/3/2000; The Guardian, 14/7/2000; The Guardian, 18/2/2000; BBC News Online, 5/9/2000]

TASK COMPLETION WISHFUL THINKING SYNDROME

¶ It's not just government and corporate managers who are inept at scheduling — it seems to be a universal human trait. In the 1990s, researchers at Sussex University conducted a five-year study into *Task Completion Wishful Thinking Syndrome* (TCWTS), which concluded that tasks always take longer than we expect. From wallpapering a room to developing a new fighter aircraft, we all tend to underestimate the duration of the jobs. We also fail to learn the lesson from previous missed deadlines.

¶ This possibly explains why, after decades of applying "advanced" management tools, there's no evidence of improvement in the scheduling profession. The 2002 international study on project management mentioned earlier (one the most comprehensive of its type) couldn't put it plainer:

> *We therefore conclude that cost underestimation has not decreased over time. Underestimation today is in the same order of magnitude as it was ten, thirty, and seventy years ago [...] No learning seems to take place in this important and highly costly sector of public and private decision making.*
> [Underestimating Costs in Public Works, Journal of the American Planning Association, Summer 2002]

GUILTY TIME-THIEVES

¶ Another aspect of TCWTS is the common feeling of accomplishing very little relative to expectations. Most workers probably feel a little guilty at five o-clock, after finishing less than half of their allotted tasks. Employers then have an easy time persuading them into working overtime. Each year employees are giving £23bn in free labour (unpaid overtime) to their bosses, according to the TUC.

¶ Some companies regard "unproductive" workers as guilty criminals. As Barbara Ehrenreich (author of *Nickel and Dimed*) noted, the retail giant Walmart calls it "time theft" when an employee "does anything other than going to the bathroom when [they're] supposed to be on company time".

¶ Meanwhile, the ambitious types who get promoted to management evidently never learn. They schedule work as if each worker is able (with the "right" motivation) to use every valuable second in productive service to the company.

RACING AGAINST THE CLOCK

¶ The view of time as a precious commodity seems to have roots in the Protestant beliefs which drove the Industrial Revolution. American business culture was the first to have workers compete against the clock to finish tasks in ever-shorter times. It was the birthplace of time-and-motion studies and Fordist assembly lines — an obsession with measuring production by stopwatch.

¶ As Charles Hampden-Turner and Fons Trompenaars point out in their book, *The Seven Cultures of Capitalism*, this obsession comes from the Puritan cultural heritage: *"The Puritans were not, like those of other religious persuasions, awaiting the afterlife in quiet contemplation. They had God's earthly kingdom to build and, given seventeenth and eighteenth-century life expectancies, a perilously short time in which to build it [...] Time is the Puritan's Great Disciplinarian and Cost Accountant"*.

¶ Hampden-Turner and Trompenaars identified two predominant cultural conceptions of time. They surveyed 15,000 managers from around the world and found that in the US, UK, Sweden and the Netherlands time is largely viewed sequentially, as a "race", whereas in Japan, Germany and France, it's conceived as a synchronised "dance".

¶ "Sequential time", they argue, is seen as a threat, as it's running out fast. The resulting anxieties lead to a preference for short-term profit-making, with paper entrepreneurs favouring creative accounting and tax avoidance over longer-term processes such as manufacturing.

¶ "Synchronised time", on the other hand, is seen as a friend. The past and future are but our memories and anticipations synchronised as ideas in the present — an eternal "dance" of possibilities recurring in the moment. Thus Japanese culture (which leans towards a synchronised view of time) tends to be the most long-term in its outlook.

¶ Short-termism in American business culture is often blamed on the higher levels of equity financing by shareholders who want quick returns. But this doesn't appear to be the real cause. Those impatient shareholders are simply reflecting existing cultural fears about time running out — the sooner they get their money, the better.

CLOCK-TIME & LIVED-TIME

¶ Bodil Jönsson, a Swedish physicist, makes a similar distinction between two ways of framing time. Her book, *Ten Thoughts about Time — a Philosophical Enquiry*, was a huge bestseller in Sweden. According to Jönsson, we divide "clock-time" into small segments in an effort to manage it, but we never feel that we have enough.

¶ Her antidote to clock-time anxiety is more "lived-time". Jönsson's two categories sound like the "sequential" and synchronised" time of Hampden-Turner. In fact both authors mention the two Greek gods of time, Chronos (god of sequential time) and Kairos (god of the opportune moment) as representative of their categories.

¶ To give an example of having more "lived-time", Jönsson describes the sense of endless expectation that children have during summer holidays. This is because they don't break it down into separate days or weeks — they see it as an undivided whole, "summer in one piece". Bodil therefore recommends a mental habit of not subdividing time.

¶ Of course, in countries such as Britain and America, with their miserly twenty-day (or less) annual holiday allowances, this will no doubt be a difficult habit to cultivate. Nothing threatens a US/UK project manager more than the idea that employees should take extended breaks whenever they feel like it. That would really screw up their project schedules.

MEASURED-TIME INSANITY

¶ In measured ("sequential" or "clock") time, the present moment is void. Only the past and future are regarded as real, as the infinitesimal point between them isn't measurable in economic terms. Time management requires us to view time in this way, and eventually it programmes our minds so that we're unable to live in the present. We're either compulsively project-ing into the future, which leads to anxiety, tension and stress — or reliving the past, which causes (in a work context) guilt, regret and resentment.

¶ The longer we spend in a time-monitored environment (eg a long-hours job) the more difficult it seems to "come to our senses" in the present moment. Presumably this is a price worth paying for the outstanding successes of government and business management. ☺

Brian Dean runs anxietyculture.com

LITTLE DEVIL GOUT

John Mitchinson discovers why no man should ever grow a beard

¶ I recently grew a beard. It wasn't planned — I'd always swore I wouldn't — but a month in the South Pacific and there it was in all its salt and pepper glory. Until a few days ago, I was all for keeping it. Now I'm not so sure. Although I can't prove what philosophers would call a necessary causal connection, the arrival of the beard is the only thing I have to explain the sudden onset of a much more unwelcome guest — gout. ¶ I can hear you laughing — go on, enjoy it, until very recently, I would have done the same. Gout is ridiculous, a kind of joke illness conjuring images of eighteenth century gluttons stretched out on couches or portly Edwardian gentlemen in wheelchairs, their lavishly bandaged feet held straight ahead of them. Portly, Edwardian gentlemen with *beards*, I feel compelled to add.¶ The reality of gout is a deal less amusing when it hits you, 'like a freight train in the night', as one of the thousands of gout-advice websites puts it. Gout pain is off the scale, mind-altering, as close as men (I imagine) get to childbirth. Even at 2,000 years distance the agony of the ancient Greek physician Aretaeus of Cappadocia is still vivid:

> Pain seizes the great toe, then the forepart of the heel on which we rest; next it comes into the arch of the foot … the ankle joint swells last of all … no other pain is more severe than this, not iron screws, nor cords, not the wound of a dagger, nor burning fire …

Thomas Sydenham, the 'English Hippocrates' was also a sufferer. Here he is in 1683:

> Now it is a violent stretching and tearing of the ligaments — now it is a gnaw-ing pain and now a pressure and tightening. So exquisite and lively meanwhile is the feeling of the part affected, that it cannot bear the weight of bedclothes nor the jar of a person walking in the room.

¶ When my attack hit one Friday evening, it chose my right ankle, rather than the more usual victim, the big toe. By midnight I was swallowing completely ineffective handfuls of Ibruprofen. By 2 am, I'd have cheerfully sawn my leg off below the knee, had I been able to stand. In the end, I spent a sleepless night, shivering (forgot to mention the fever), wiggling my toes at the bedroom wall, which was the only thing that brought any relief. Exhausted and depressed (gout and melancholy are first cousins), I spent the next morning educating myself on

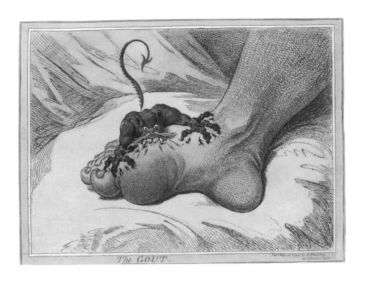

The GOUT.

what Edward Gibbon once called, in that annoyingly self-important 18th century way, the 'honourable enemy'. I much prefer his contemporary, James Gilray's vision of gout as a pocket-sized Satan, breathing fire from his nostrils while sinking sharp teeth and claws into a poor unfortunate's foot.¶ Gibbon's point, I suppose, was that if you're going to suffer from anything, then gout — or the gout — carries an impressive cachet. Not only is it ancient (the earliest recorded gout victim is a 5,000 year old Egyptian mummy) for centuries it was seen as mark of breeding, the disease of kings, a by-product of high living, high intelligence and sexual libertinism. The list of gout sufferers reads like a roll-call of western civilisation: Alexander the Great, Kubla Khan, Henry VIII, Martin Luther, John Milton, Sir Isaac Newton, Louis XIV, Benjamin Franklin, Thomas Jefferson, William Penn, Jonathan Swift, Dr Johnson, Charles Darwin, William Morris, Joseph Conrad, Pablo Neruda. Falstaff, my absolute favourite Shakespeare character had gout; in fact, if you were an educated, successful, lively white male who liked a drink, prior to the Second World War, gout appeared to be an accident waiting to happen. For a few moments, I felt a sudden flush of pride — my ankle was transformed into an object of historical curiosity. But the consolations of history are fleeting, particularly when your foot feels like its being rolled backwards and forwards in mangle and soon I was plunged back into the horrible medical details.¶ Was gout really just the payback for being a clever, fat, greedy bastard? If only life was so straightforward. Gout is caused by the excessive production of uric acid in the blood. Needle-sharp crystals form around your joints, sending your white blood cells into overdrive, leading to a huge build-up of fluid. Uric acid is for the most part, a benign waste product created when the body breaks down the purines which make up the genetic material in plant and animal cells. Things can go wrong when we eat too much purine-rich food but — rather appropriately given that purines actually make our genes — the metabolic malfunction that causes gout is an inherited condition. Eating the wrong food and drinking too much just act as the trigger.¶ I can't say I drew much comfort from this. Whatever causes it, once you've got it, you've got for life. Gout, basically a form of arthritis, is incurable. But you can't ignore it:

> Gout will get progressively worse without treatment, attacking more and more frequently and severely and involving more joints until a chronic condition of gout occurs. Chronic gout causes damage to the joints, crippling and disability.

Great. It's also an early indicator of heart disease, often leads to kidney stones and sometimes causes painful chalky lumps called tophi to grow on the affected joints. The gout devil demands management, which basically means controlling what you eat and drinking as little alcohol as you can get away with. Here's what's on the menu:

> White bread and cereal
> Skim milk
> Fizzy drinks
> Soup without meat stock
> Lo-fat cheese
> Sugar
> Pasta and macaroni
> Peanut butter

Now here's the verboten list:

> Anchovies, herring, mackerel, sardines
> Bacon, salami, sausages generally
> Broths and gravies
> Game – goose, duck, partridge
> Caviar and roe
> Liver, kidneys, offal generally
> Scallops and mussels
> Beer – never, ever, ever.

¶ In a way, this made it easy. I live 27 steps from one of the best real ale pubs in England. I keep my own pigs, and make my own bacon, salami and sausages.

My 'way' with offal has been praised by Jonathan Meades, the greatest restaurant critic of this or any age. My kitchen is a shrine to the works of Hugh Fearnley-Whittingstall and Fergus Henderson. My best friend describes me as 'a man with a flagon in one hand and a pie in the other.' To hell with this, I thought. I can't live on a chav diet of fizzy drinks and white bread (it turns out that fizzy drinks had that very day been outed as a gout risk). I can't face a life without roast partridge, devilled kidneys or nutty, hoppy pints of Exmoor Gold. Like Nick Cage's leather jacket in *Wild at Heart*, good food and drink was 'a symbol of my individuality and my belief in personal freedom'. What are 'food guidelines' anyway, except self-contradictory arse-covering by the medical establishment? ¶ By the third day, the painkillers seemed to have tamed the foot-devil so I hobbled to the pub, downed a couple of celebratory pints, had a large Bruichladdich with my dad and returned home to feast on pheasant and pig's trotter pie. Despite my high spirits, this proved a big mistake. At midnight it was as though someone had turned on the boiling-hot pain valve in my ankle, which in a sense they — or I — had. ¶ Pain is a great leveller and an even better teacher. After my long night of remorse, I got some serious pain killers and made some serious plans. The beer would have to go — it turns out to little more than purine soup, alas — but red-wine-in-moderation sneaks in under the low purine-wire. Also, a family friend (an Oxford don, of course: high table must be like a gout veterans drop-in centre) came up with a painless way of getting the uric acid level down. It seems the anti-oxidant chemical in red cherries (anthocyanin: the same stuff that makes autumn leaves turn red) does the trick, and tastes rather nicer than shark cartilage or nettles which are also touted as alternatives. Better still, a company in Middlesex called Cherry Active have found away of compressing half a tree of cherries into a single bottle and supplying them by mail, so I'm sorted for a while. I'll eat less of the food I love, and try hard not to get shitfaced. At the first twinge, I'll start necking the cherry juice. But best of all, in what feels like a reward for my week of torment and self-induced shame, I discover that there's something else that speeds the passage of uric acid through the body. Regular sex. I read the highly reputable medical website several times, but there it is in black and white. *Sex prevents gout.* My foot throbs with excitement. My entirely blameless beard bristles with anticipation. Cometh the malady; cometh the cure. Life may never be the groaning banquet it once was but it may yet turn out to be a bowl of cherries. 🐚

Some useful websites and sources: www.gouteducation.org www.cherryactive.co.uk
Roy Porter & G.S. Rousseau, Gout: *The Patrician Malady* (Yale)

QI IDLE ANIMALS

Can any animal really qualify as an idler? Surely they are continually driven into non-stop activity by their need to eat and reproduce? Far less than you'd think, as it turns out.

¶ Obviously, the sloth family is in a league of its own: no other mammal is lazy enough to allow algae to grow on their fur, nor survive on a digestion so painfully slow that they can actually starve to death on a full stomach. But there are plenty of other animal sluggards, some of them rather surprising:

Bees

Despite their reputation, honey bees aren't all that busy. They look it, buzzing from flower to flower, and we all are dead impressed by the fact that single bee would have to travel the equivalent of twice around the world to make a pound of honey, but they don't. They might spend a couple of weeks on serious pollen duty, usually towards the end of their life; the rest of the time, they're hanging out around the hive, growing, or feeding the next generation and they all take a six month winter break. Nice work if you can get it.

Beavers

Beavers are slightly busier than bees, but a five hour day is about the limit. During the winter they leave their lodge only once a fortnight, sustained by a larder of logs and the fat stored in their scaly tails. In 1760, the odd texture of their tails led the College of Physicians and Faculty of Divinity in Paris to classify the beaver as a fish. This meant the French settlers in North America could officially eat beaver during Lent and on other fast days. Beaver tail is supposed to taste like roast beef.

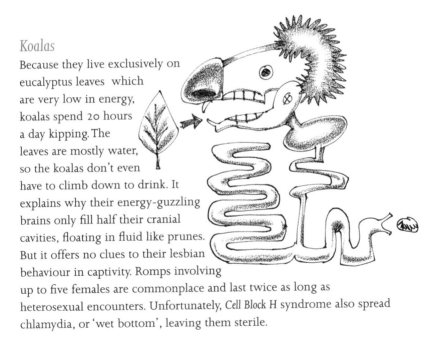

Koalas

Because they live exclusively on eucalyptus leaves which are very low in energy, koalas spend 20 hours a day kipping. The leaves are mostly water, so the koalas don't even have to climb down to drink. It explains why their energy-guzzling brains only fill half their cranial cavities, floating in fluid like prunes. But it offers no clues to their lesbian behaviour in captivity. Romps involving up to five females are commonplace and last twice as long as heterosexual encounters. Unfortunately, *Cell Block H* syndrome also spread chlamydia, or 'wet bottom', leaving them sterile.

Tuataras

This ancient New Zealander is are the most primitive
of all living reptiles. Their brain is tiny and their heart
and circulatory system are rudimentary, making them
extremely cold-blooded. 'Do it slowly' is the tuatara's
motto. They can live for over a century but it takes
them 15 years to reach sexual maturity and the females
only squeeze out an egg every four years. They 'hunt'
by sitting outside their burrows waiting for beetles,
worms, or better still, of a young tuatara to toddle past.
To defend themselves they sit inside their burrows,
waiting for the danger to go: hardly a challenge for
a sprightly rat.

Sea Cows

Sea cows — manatees and dugongs — are more closely
related to elephants than cows, but they have a very laid-back life.
They paddle around in warm tropical seas, with little
competition for food and no natural predators.
When they aren't eating or sleeping, sea cows
come together regularly to 'cavort'. These
sessions of nuzzling, bumping, kissing, and
mutual masturbation can involve up to four
individuals of either sex and last for several
hours. Interestingly, their louche lifestyle
seems to have left them impervious
to the diseases which afflict other
mammals, like cancer and
syphilis, propelling
them to the forefront
of medical research.

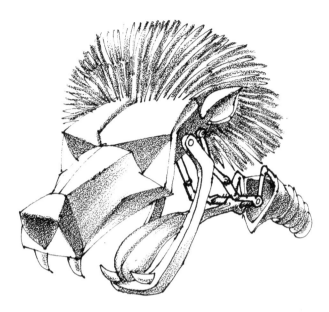

Lions

While it's pretty stressful being a young lion—constant battles for supremacy, insatiable lionesses—in general, mature male lions are loafers. Lionesses and hyenas do most of the actual killing; even the big dark manes are a con. Far from being an indicator of virility, they are the leonine version of the hair that sprouts from the ears and nostrils of middle-aged men. Worse still, a lazy old lion is much more likely to turn man-eater. Slow, weak and always hanging around, we are easy prey: the lion's equivalent of a night in watching telly with beer and a pizza.

Meet other bone idle beasts in the pages of The QI Book of Animal Ignorance *by John Lloyd & John Mitchinson (Faber & Faber).*
Illustrations by Ted Dewan.

The Wit and Wisdom of
ANDY WARHOL

Paul Hamilton covers himself in tin-foil screaming, "whip me bitch!"

¶ America has always been utterly bereft of artists — people who can actually paint and draw and sculpt — but abundant with art collectors. The post-WWII American administration didn't like all their dollars disappearing overseas to patronize European artists and galleries, so it was decided that a new and wholly American artform be created to reverse the trend. Thus the CIA-backed school of Abstract Expressionism was born, a style of painting that required no skill in composition, drawing, perspective or even the ability to mix colours. Jackson Pollock dripped paint from buckets over horizontal

canvasses, Willem De Kooning pushed paint around canvasses with a broom, making infantile bug-eyed faces. Of course, it was peddled as The Angry Youth Of America Reacting To The Post-War World, every splatter and dribble indicative of the artists' inarticulate horror and revulsion, every brushmark torn screaming from their sensitive, tortured souls. And then came Andy Warhol, a graphic designer making good money drawing shoes and cats for fashion magazines. Andy desperately wanted to be taken seriously as an artist. The problem was he lacked the requisite rage and the compulsory macho Alpha Male hard-drinking misogynist sensibility to attack a picture like the Abstract Boys. He was a shy, withdrawn bag of homosexual nerves with a side order of premature baldness, fucked skin, dyslexia and Asperger's Syndrome to go. So, rather than rail against the world he celebrated it in all its horrific glory by making Brillo Pad boxes that were exactly like the real thing, paintings of Campbell's Soup tins, silkscreen portraits of tragic heroines like Marilyn Monroe, Elizabeth Taylor and Jackie Onassis, multiple images of car crash photos and electric chairs. When asked why he made masses of copies of a silkscreened portrait rather than one single oil painting, Andy disarmingly and honestly answered, 'It's easy.' What was refreshing and vital about Warhol the Pop Artist was his demolition of the pretentious image of the solitary poet artist suffering in penury to create his art. Andy had plenty of assistants helping him make his pictures, the pictures themselves taken from newspapers and film magazines. The subject matter of his pictures were suggested by colleagues like New York art maven Henry Geldzahler. He was rarely present for the filming of his own movies, films that had so little in terms of camera movement that he called them 'stillies'. Never before had an artist been so absent from his own work. Was he a visionary, a philosopher, the living mirror of the emotionally-empty consumer age — or an idiot-savant who got lucky? Artistic or autistic? True, he supported and nurtured The Velvet Underground but let's not forget he loved Duran Duran and Curiosity Killed The Cat, too. ¶ The following selection of Warhol musings on life and how to live it, mainly collected from the Sixties and Seventies, will tell you everything and nothing.

AVOIDING THE VOID

I'm sure I'm going to look in the mirror and see nothing. People are always calling me a mirror and if a mirror looks into a mirror, what is there to see?

THAT QUOTE

In the future everyone will be world famous for 15 minutes. (1968)

I'm bored with that line. I never use it anymore. My new line is, "In fifteen minutes everybody will be famous." (1979)

SPOT: THE DIFFERENCE

If the pimple on my upper right cheek is gone, a new one turns up on my lower left cheek, on my jawline, near my ear, in the middle of my nose, under the hair on my eyebrows, right between my eyes. I think it's the same pimple, moving from place to place ... If someone asked me, "What's your problem?" I'd have to say, "Skin."

PIESOLATION

I really like to eat alone. I want to start a chain of restaurants for other people who are like me called ANDY-MATS — The Restaurant For The Lonely Person. You get your food and then you take your tray into a booth and watch television.

FILM

The best atmosphere I can think of is film, because it's three-dimensional physically and two-dimensional emotionally.

All my films are artificial but then everything is sort of artificial, I don't know where the artificial stops and the real starts.

And I'm most concerned with, uh ... doing bad camerawork and, uh ... ah ... and we're trying to make it so bad but doing it well.

If I ever had to cast an acting role, I want the wrong person for the part. I can never visualize the right person in a part. The right person for the right part would be too much. Besides, no person is ever completely right for any part, so if you can't get someone who's perfectly right, it's more satisfying to get someone's who's perfectly wrong. Then you know you've really got something.

I don't know, it's so easy to do movies, I mean you can, uh ... uh ... just shoot and every picture comes out right.

What I was actually trying to do in my early movies was show how people can meet other people and what they can do and what they can say to each other ... Those movies showed you how some people act and react with other people. They were like actual sociological "For instances." They were like documentaries, and if you thought it could apply to you, it was an example, and if it didn't apply to you, at least it was a documentary.

ON "SLEEP", HIS THREE-HOUR FILM OF JOHN GIORNO SLEEPING

Seeing everybody up all the time made me think that sleep was becoming pretty obsolete, so I decided I'd better quickly do a movie of a person sleeping.

MULTI-TASKING

Maybe the reason my memory is so bad is that I always do at least two things at once. It's easier to forget something you only half-did or quarter-did.

My favourite simultaneous action is talking while eating. I think it's a sign of class. The rich have many advantages over the poor but the most important one, as far as I'm concerned, is knowing how to talk and eat at the same time. [...] At dinner you're expected to eat — because if you don't it's an insult to the hostess — and you're expected to talk — because if you don't it's an insult to the other guests. The rich somehow manage to work it out but I just can't do it. They are never caught with an open mouth full of food but [it's] always my turn to talk just when I've filled my mouth with mashed potatoes ... I practice at home in front of the mirror and over the phone. In the meantime, until I've perfected the ability to talk and eat simultaneously, I stick to my basic rule for dinner party behaviour; don't talk and don't eat.

THE WARHOL CURE-ALL

Sometimes people let the same problem make them miserable for years when they could just say, "So what?" That's one of my favourite things to say. "So what?"

"My mother didn't love me." So what?

"My husband won't ball me." So what?

"I'm a success but I'm still alone." So what?

I don't know how I made it through all the years before I learned how to do that trick. It took a long time to learn it, but once you do, you never forget.

ANDY HAS A LINE

People say "time on my hands". Well, I looked at my hands and I saw a lot of lines. And then somebody told me that some people don't have lines. I didn't believe her. We were sitting in a restaurant and she said, "How can you say that? Look at that waiter over there!" She called him over, "Honey! Honey? Can you bring me a glass of water?" and when he brought it she grabbed his hand and showed it to me and it had no lines! Just the three main ones. And she said, "See? I told you. Some people like that waiter have no lines." And I thought, "Gee, I wish I was a waiter."

ANDY ON COKE

What's great about this country is that America started the tradition where the richest consumers buy essentially the same things as the poorest. You can be watching TV and see Coca-Cola, and you can know that the President drinks Coke, Liz Taylor drinks Coke, and just think, you can drink Coke, too. A Coke is a Coke and no amount of money can get you a better Coke than the one the bum on the corner is drinking. All the Cokes are the same and all the Cokes are good. Liz Taylor knows it, the President knows it, the bum knows it, and you know it.

WORK

I suppose I have a really loose interpretation of "work" because I think that just being alive is so much work at something you don't always want to do. Being born is like being kidnapped. And then being sold into slavery. People are working every minute. The machinery is always going. Even when you sleep.

THE AGE-OLD PROBLEM

I decided to go gray so nobody would know how old I was and I would look younger to them than how old they thought I was. I would gain a lot by going gray:
1) I would have "old" problems, which were easier to take than "young" problems, 2) everyone would be impressed by how young I looked, and 3) I would be relieved of the responsibility of acting young — I could occasionally lapse into eccentricity or senility and no-one would think anything of it because of my gray hair. When you've got gray hair, every move you make seems "young" and "spry" instead of just being normally active. It's like you're getting a new talent. So I dyed my hair gray when I was about twenty-three or twenty-four.

CHANGING DULLER

I love every "lib" [i.e. liberation] movement there is, because after the "lib" the things that were always a mystique become understandable and boring, and then nobody has to feel left out if they're not part of what is happening.

ART

I can never get over when you're on the beach how beautiful the sand looks and the water washes it away and straightens it up and the trees and the grass all look great. I think having land and not ruining it is the most beautiful art that anybody could ever want to own.

Why do people think artists are special? It's just another job.

CRITICAL NUMBERS

Don't pay any attention to what they write about you. Just measure it in inches.

In some circles where very heavy people think they have very heavy brains, words like "charming" and "clever" and "pretty" are all put-downs; all the lighter things in life, which are the most important things, are put down

SELFISH

I'm a deeply superficial person.

If you want to know all about Andy Warhol, just look at the surface of my paintings and films and there I am. There's nothing behind it.

Cash. I just am not happy when I don't have it. The minute I have it I have to spend it. And I just buy STUPID THINGS.

My mind always drifts when I hear words like "objective" or "subjective" — I never know what people are talking about. I just don't have the brains.

Really, what is life about? You get sick and die. That's it. So you've just got to keep busy.

I'm not disciplined, really. It just looks that way because I do what people tell me to do.

LOVE

Two people kissing always look like fish.

When I look around today, the biggest anachronism I see is pregnancy. I just can't believe that people are still pregnant.

The biggest price you pay for love is that you have to have somebody around, you can't be on your own, which is always so much better. The biggest disadvantage, of course, is no room in bed.

THE TIES THEY ARE A-CHANGING

I was trying to think the other day about what you do now in America if you want to be successful. Before, you were dependable and wore a good suit. Looking around, I guess that today you have to do all the same things but not wear a good suit. I guess that's all it is. Think rich. Look poor.

If a person isn't generally considered beautiful, they can still be a success if they have a few jokes in their pockets. And a lot of pockets. ☻

THE GOVERNMENT GUIDE TO

SOCIAL SCRUTINY

IDENTITY THEFT

A Department of Social Scrutiny Infoganda leaflet
channelled by Ian Vince • www.socialscrutiny.org

The Department of Social Scrutiny (DoSS) would like to announce the opening of its brand new Identity Theft Centre – a state-of-the-art facility built to allay any fears you may have regarding the security of data we hold about you, the hapless, average person on the street.

From today, all of your information will be held on computer at a central facility, the location of which is secret, except to staff who were specially picked to work there for their distrustful and paranoiac dispositions. As part of its recruitment drive, DoSS agents planted messages in every domestic refuse sack in the UK – so, if you did not think to go through your bin for secret messages from the government, then we are sorry, but you are far too mentally stable to work for us.

Below: An artist's impression of the top secret Identity Theft Centre, drawn up from leaked blueprints found in the back of a TNT van.

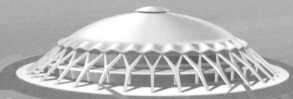

About our staff

The Identity Theft Centre is guarded by private contractors wearing fancy dress police uniform and expressions of hateful melancholy that put off even authorised visitors, let alone trespassers.

Housed in Portakabins around the site, the guards – each of which is trained in anger mismanagement – are piped a sophisticated system of 24 hour CCTV and Sky Sports monitoring, along with subliminal, hurtful insinuations about their sexual prowess.

IAN VINCE

DATA SECURITY BREACHES
What You Can Do to Protect Yourself From Us

In the light of recent security breaches, The Department of Social Scrutiny (DoSS) has issued the following guidance on the subject of Identity Theft (IT) on behalf of The Government.

PROTECTING YOUR COMPROMISED IDENTITY

 You should, without delay, change your date of birth. This has the added advantage of enabling you to pick a more suitable star sign than the one you already have.

 Alter your mother's maiden name and gender. This is complex, but does at least stop family historians in their tracks and will lead to the eventual destruction of the genealogy industry.

 Instruct your bank, building society and any other financial institution to write to you in invisible ink, Icelandic runes or the secret code of the Puffin Club.

 As a precautionary measure, step up your rigorous online security regime by altering all of your web site passwords from "password" to "newpassword".

 Obtain a new personality. You will be given an application form for this after your next round of Electro-Convulsive Therapy, free for everyone who finds living in Britain a little depressing. You may elect to choose a green electricity supplier upon payment of a small premium.

by Tony Husband

BILL AND ZED'S BAD ADVICE

We've fucked up our lives. Now it's your turn.

❖

Dear Bill and Zed,

The other night I was with my new lady friend, a statuesque and beautiful Finn. However, on retiring to the boudoir, she put on a Rod Stewart CD. Now, I have put up with her shocking musical taste with good grace but this was the last straw. I gently said, "no, sorry," and asked her to remove the CD. She grumbled a bit but obliged. The only problem is that hearing "I Am Sailing" even for only a few seconds gave me a soft-on for the rest of the night. I mean, I never liked Rod Stewart much before but now I know he can cause impotence I fucking LOATHE him. But what can I do about the girl's music collection? These days it's not like you can torch it, most of it's on the net. Can one re-educate a woman in this matter?

Yours
KB, London

ZED: Dear KB,

If I was banging some Scandinavian chick up the jacksie in my ex-wife's house she could play Judas Priest, I wouldnt even hear it. Stop moaning you idiot and get her pregnant, then you can leave her. Heh, heh, heres to crime.

BILL: Well KB,

For you I'm going to step out of the construct that is my persona for this rather predictable column and tell you that I only have to hear any Rod Stewart record from the past 37 years and counting and I instantly think of Mary McElwee. She was a girl that I had a huge crush on in my teenage years. Maggie May was playing on the jukebox in the Nags Head, Corby when I first noticed her. Also it was Mary McElwee who subsequently educated me to the glories of *Astral Weeks*, *Saint Dominic's Preview* and *Veedon Fleece*. So don't give me that fucking "re-educate a woman in this matter" line. You're the one that needs re-educating. As for Bad Advice, I wouldn't deign to give you any even if my life depended on it. As for Mary McElwee, I hope her life has been happy and rewarding.

Dear Bill and Zed,

As a long-term married man I find my life becoming somewhat dull and predictable. Should I perhaps embark on a discreet affair or two, or perhaps cultivate a drug habit? Or perhaps both? I'm not getting any younger, you know.

Yours,
Bored, Cirencester

ZED: Dear Mr Cirencester,

Affairs? Drugs? Both are delicious distractions and can ruin one's life spectacularly before you even realise the party's over. However, if spectacular self-immolation and possible incarceration is more your bag, why not try visiting teenage chatrooms and making a few little cyber chums. I recommend www.cyberjailbait.com. Some real little honeys on that one.

BILL: Dear Bored,

The only thing that is dull and predictable is you. Discreet affairs and drug habits are about as dull and predictable as it gets. I recommend you get a Jiffy bag, stamp it and then address it to a girl you once knew, then phone 999 and ask for an ambulance. While waiting for it to arrive get your Stanley knife and cut off your cock. Put the cock in the Jiffy and seal it. On your way to the hospital in the ambulance, ask if they can pull up at a letterbox and one of them can drop your small package into the slot. That my friend would be neither dull nor predictable.

Dear Bill and Zed,

Following some perhaps ill-starred advice from an agony uncle, I recently started doing a little cheating on the missus and hoovering up a bit of the old Colombian sherbert. Unfortunately, her indoors has started intercepting my phone bills and checking all my emails. Should I knuckle under to this Stasi-like regime or just give her a playful slapping and tell her to fuck off, this is just the kind of thing that puts a bit of zip into a marriage?

Yours

Tarquin Cheese-Knife, Woking

ZED: Dear Tarquin,

Fuck the slapping, fuck the phone bills, fuck the wife. Why not beat the bitch to the punch and simply fuck off yourself? Tell her she can keep the phone, keep the keys, keep the house, keep the the bills, keep the kids. You're going to Thailand to find yourself a fine young ladyboy who understands you.

That should shut her up.

BILL: Dear Tarquin,

Well, obviously you got your advice from the wrong agony uncles. Ours is always solid gold easy action. But it is not for me to besmirch any of our rivals. If ladyboys are not to your taste, why not head to South America where you will find both women and drugs cheap? Once there you can spend the rest of your life wallowing in guilt and regret.

Dear Bill and Zed,

After taking some possibly ill-thought-out advice in this appalling magazine recently, my wife has thrown me out of home and changed all the locks. I thought the best way of dealing with this would be to write a sitcom for the BBC about two divorced fathers forced to live together by their ex-wives. We got a standard letter back from the BBC telling us that they no longer accept, or even read, scripts from men about the mid-life crisis. So we realised we need what TS Eliot called an objective correlative, a metaphor which would address the situation obliquely. I thought of having a policeman in a coma thinking it's 1973, but apparently that's already been done. Any ideas?

Yours

Michael Suicide, Bridgend

ZED: Dear Michael,

How about two totally irresponsible, retired rockstars who kill their wives and go to Thailand on a sex and murder spree and end up on Thailand's death row? Lots of laughs there.

A bit like Porridge only with loads of hilarious buggery jokes and horrendous sexual violence gags.

Sounds like a winner to me.

I'm sure those sweary, cutting edge Channel Four boffs would love it.

BILL: Dear Micky,

The advice that you have already been given by Z is perfect in almost every way, except, why live life vicariously? Fuck the writing a sitcom bit and get yourself over to Thailand and start your own murder spree. To spend the rest of one's days on death row would give every moment of what remains of your life a vitality that you will never get in Bridgend or even Hoxton.

CONVERSATIONS

John Lloyd and John Mitchinson

We can't stand around here doing nothing, people will think we're workmen. SPIKE MILLIGAN

QUITE INTERESTING CONVERSATION

Tom Hodgkinson meets QI's John Lloyd and John Mitchinson,
mortal foes of boredom, anger and authority

One of the symptoms of an approaching nervous breakdown is the belief that one's work is terribly important. BERTRAND RUSSELL

BEHIND QI THE TELLY SHOW AND BOOKS, THERE IS A SERIOUS philosophical remit: to end boredom and to rethink the way we learn. Here the two Johns dicuss work, play, the horrors of school and the redeeming power of curiosity.

LLOYD: I'll tell you a funny thing about work. I met this guy, a school gate Dad, just when we were beginning to do QI, at a dinner party and I was telling this group of six or eight people what QI did. This hedge fund guy, with billions in the bank, having decided to sell his business and retire at forty, leapt to his feet and shouted, "how dare you try and tell me what I find interesting! You're a cultural fascist!" and I said, "sorry, Jeremy, what?" And he ran off into the garden. He came back and said, "I'm sorry, it's just that ever since I gave up work I don't know what to do with myself." He went back and started up another hedge fund and he's much happier. Getting the 6.30 train and making shed loads of money, because then he doesn't have to think about what matters. For some people work is an absolute crutch. I know because I gave up working. It was one of the things that triggered off the crisis that started QI. I was forty-two. I said to my wife Sarah, "My life

is so meaningless, so pointless, I'm so dull, I don't know anything. All I know is how to make television commercials about banks and lager. I've got to take some time off, I've got no ideas, I've got to recharge my batteries." So I took three months off, and it was the most horrific experience, Tom, because I could do what I wanted but I didn't know what to do. I used to wander up and down the Fulham Road and think, maybe I should get a job as a waiter and not tell Sarah, you know, and tell her I'm relaxing, but work really really hard in someone's kitchen. And I went on an art class, I thought I must learn to do something proper, something meaningful. I went to this art class at Chelsea College of Art, and I walked in and someone said, "what are you doing here?" I said, "well I've come to learn to draw," and she said, "I've seen you on telly, why would you want to learn to draw here? In this terrible dump?" I did four of these weeks of classes, and she was really horrible to me, she said, "can't you see? Can't you see that the pomegranate should be next to the orange? What's the matter with you?"

IDLER: What was wrong with her?

JL: I don't know, she was pissed off, in a dead end job, a lot of teachers are. They won't sit still, they won't let me just get through the hours. But it's like in life, the problems are the opportunities, as is often said. The difficult bits show you the way to something different and often so much better. Difficult children are a nightmare for schools so they think, let's just expel this person, because they're always late and they don't do up their tie. It's not, hang on, this person has got a really odd way of looking at things.

IDLER: So QI really does have a radical centre.

MITCHINSON: What I think starts off with kangaroo's vaginas and the wives of Henry VIII ends up with trying to figure out why you're here. Because once you start to ask questions ...

IDLER: We can definitely philosophise about why we are here, but aren't you also attacking the *status quo* in terms of the Government, business and so on?

JL: It's not really about attacking people and certainly not individuals. It's about making people see there's a more interesting angle of looking at things. And actually, the research makes you very much less judgmental about things. I spend a lot of time researching tribes and languages in West Africa and I think to most people West Africa is "well, they're very black aren't they?" and they all speak a bit like Idi Amin. It's hot and sweaty and there are mosquitos, rainforests and Nigeria is very corrupt and that's about it really. They don't know that

there are 500 ethnic groups in Nigeria alone. All the ships in the Nigerian navy are called hippopotamus, but they're all in different languages ...

IDLER: What I'm trying to say is those of us who learn about the world from newspapers and teachers are not told these things. But isn't there a reason why we're not told these things?

JL: There isn't an evil lord running the CIA. That person, no matter how evil they appear to be, is just struggling through life. What we're trying to get round to is that if everyone was really interested and curious there wouldn't be these problems.

JM: These people would be a lot less powerful. I mean I think now, in general, people are a lot less able to put up with politics, people are ignoring it as irrelevant and not being to do with them addressing their lives.

IDLER: When did it though? Did people ever think it was relevant?

JL: They were more interested.

JM: At the end of the Second World War a lot of people voted for Labour to get Churchill out.

IDLER: I think people were interested in the 18th Century, because you could actually see Pitt or John Wilkes walking down the road.

JL: The Romans had no word for "interesting", did you know that? Or "boring" for that matter. The Industrial Revolution is about the time we get the words boring and boredom. It's work-related. When work is repetitive, meaningless, pointless, badly paid and dangerous, you need a word for this feeling that you get. As an agricultural worker, it may be very hard work but you've got the seasons, you actually know a lot about lambs and potatoes, so you don't need a word for interesting because it's what you

My grandfather once told me that there are two kinds of people: those who do the work and those who take the credit. He told me to try to be in the first group; there was less competition there.

INDIRA GANDHI

do. This is the worky feeling, boring. Do you know the derivation of noise? Noise comes from "nausea" and what "nausea" means is the feeling you get on a ship, naus means ship, so nausea is that shippy feeling. So the Greeks had this thing where the feeling of what you got on a ship was "er, oh dear …" disturbance, very uncomfortable. From that you get noise, which is a particular kind of uncomfortable feeling. Because there wasn't much noise of that kind, unless you were in a battle or a volcano blew up. They didn't have the kind of noise that we put up with everyday.

JM: We still have "noisome" which means irritating. But I mean … going back to work, there is the division between work and play, which is very strict in our culture. I'm absolutely sure that most of the creative work people do comes through the play state, not the work state. You need to be able to focus to get things done. But the creative state is when you're in that reflective state.

IDLER: The Yequana Indians don't even have a word for work. One has started to come in, *trabaja*, from the Spanish but they don't have one in their own language.

JM: The French word *travaille* comes from the word for torture …

IDLER: … but the idea of work for them meaning "a regrettable necessity" does not exist. It's all mixed up together.

JM: In most hunter gatherer societies very, very little work gets done.

IDLER: But lots of philosophizing.

JL: There was this fantastic organisation I came across once called the Liberty Fund. There was this guy, in the 1920s, who was in agribusiness, and he had a huge fortune. He had an intuition just before the great crash in 1929 that it was all going to go wrong. So he

sold all his stocks and then it all fell and of course he found he was the richest man in the Universe. And his hobby was philosophy. He loved to talk philosophy. He couldn't stand other billionaires because billionaires are only interested in money, and yachts and stuff. So in order to get people to talk to he had to create this organisation and he paid people to be his chat friends. So he set up this Liberty Fund thing, and now it's a huge organisation and they run about 200 seminars all around the world every year. They pay you a thousand dollars and set you up in a nice hotel and then send you some reading material. Anyway I did it and I got sent *No Logo* and some Spinoza. There's always fourteen people. You sit around a table and there's a chairman who might be some wonderful Philosophy professor, like Steve Erickson, and he leads the discussion. And you sit there and talk, for no reason at all, about these interesting things. And over these three days you make friends for life. And you learn the most amazing amount, it's a wonderful thing. And these fourteen people, I could go to war with them. They are wonderful people. And he starts by saying, "you probably all think this is some CIA plot but it isn't. It's completely and genuinely for the sake of itself." That's what we should be doing. I spent a day researching on Saturday, and John's the same, and you spend the whole day completely absorbed in discovery. You learn lots of new things. Like the fact that the white cliffs of Dover are made out of plankton. It's fascinating, and yet most people spend Saturday afternoon being bored, or angry, and it's a crime!

IDLER: Do you think your TV show has that effect on people, does it stimulate a new way of looking at things, and a new interest in learning?

JL: No, what's really weird is we get no letters, maybe one a week if we're lucky. Almost no feedback. Very, very little. It's very odd. It's the way the establishment always gets rid of rebellion. It's by promoting it. That's what happens at public school. You get the worst boys and make them prefects.

JM: It's like Oxford and Cambridge, you get the brightest people, give them somewhere nice to live, give them nice food, and they think: this is great.

IDLER: You do get lots of radical professors at University though. I had at least one.

JL: There are actually very few successful radical professors at University now. I would say there are no millionaire professors who are radical. It's like comedians. They all start off, Ben Elton, Billy Connolly, having a go at the Government but a few years later they start saying, "Oh no, I never had a go at Margaret Thatcher, I quite like Mrs T.," and now you've got Billy Connolly, friend of the Royal family. These people are promoted out of danger so that they don't rock the system. And in many ways that's what happening to QI. We're getting very successful so we aren't seen as radical any more.

JM: Politicians, actors, comedians, priests— they're all doing the same kind of job. They are performers and they're playing roles. You believe in their performance but you'd be mistaken to believe what they were saying was actually true. What these people say up on stage isn't what they believe when they're at home eating their toast.

IDLER: So how do you stop yourself becoming a caricature of your own work?

JL: It is very difficult. When Douglas Adams was at the height of his fame he was very, very unhappy, very confused. He wrote these wonderful things with his great sense of humour and then he became all the people he parodied. Immensely rich and rather pompous. Mel and Griff did a wonderful parody of *Hitchhiker*, brilliantly accurate, pointing out that all the things he'd made jokes about, he'd become. He got really upset about it. Really, really angry.

IDLER: I think Lennon did it quite well, he continued to be radical.

JL: Do you remember how much people used to mock him for marrying Yoko and baking bread and all that stuff. You look at it now and he was right.

JM: Why is it that so many people dislike John Lennon? Self-righteous, preachy...

IDLER: I think people find it hard to deal with the apparent contradictions. Playing "Imagine" in his mansion.

JL: You know people say "champagne socialist", well, so what? You'd rather people were champagne fascists would you? Surely it's a good thing? It's better to give something back than keep it all to yourself.

IDLER: Have you read *The Man Who Was Thursday* by G.K. Chesterton? It's about a group of anarchists and these two guys are having this terrific row about the state of society and then one of them takes them down to this cellar café and says, "oh they do a wonderful Chablis here."

JM: I like proper old-fashioned anarchism — persistent refusal to sign up ... I certainly don't feel able to sign up to any political party at the moment. I hate this thing "millions of people have died to sacrifice themselves for your right to vote ..." No, actually, they sacrificed themselves for all sorts of reasons.

The world's most dangerous jobs are agriculture, mining and construction.

The single most dangerous specific job is said to be that of Alaskan crab fishermen working in the Bering Sea.

JL: It is tricky, if you can't vote for anyone, again it's a very QI thing. It's because they don't have any interesting ideas. They don't. And they are all trying to guess what we want. Which is the other disaster of our culture. Instead of saying this and this should happen because it would be a great idea.

IDLER: It's ridiculous. If you'd asked people in a poll in 1962 "what would you most like to appear in popular music?" no one would have said, "four slightly long haired men from Liverpool".

JM: Futurologists predicted that the world would run out of food so they got that wrong because now there's too much food, but we can't get it to the people that need it, but no-one predicted the Internet. It was all people living on Mars ...

IDLER: They're still going on about that though. Some of these futurologists running Facebook and all the rest have these ideas about going to Mars and living for a thousand years.

JL: Even today the Internet seems, even though it's annoying sometimes when you can't log on in one second, utterly miraculous.

JM: Well, what is miraculous, I think, is that the breakthrough in the technology came to saints. Tim Berners Lee could be the richest man that has ever lived but instead he decided that he wanted it to be free. I get rather bored by the sandal-wearing Internet hippies saying no one should make any money from the Internet because that's never going to happen, but it is true that it is mostly extraordinary. It does undermine a lot of greed.

IDLER: I think it stops people though. I mean instead of going on a march or attemptng to recreate their everyday lives and deslave themselves, people are putting stuff up on Facebook ...

JM: I really think this social networking stuff is going to collapse under its own weight.

IDLER: But it has 60 million people and it's going up all the time

JM: But of those 60 million 40 million probably hardly ever use it and think it's a load of shit. But who is "the man", do you think, now? You know, "working for the man" It's really hard to know who "the man" is. Is it global capitalism? Well, sort of.

IDLER: It's the man inside you.

JL: The man in your head is doing all the controlling, far more than MI5 or the CIA.

IDLER: There is stuff going on though. The word "Papist" as in "Papist Plot" was completely invented by the Elizabethans as a way of promoting Protestantism. It's like Newspeak. The authorities change the language in order to condition us.

JM: Like Al-Quaeda, we're all experts about Al-Quaeda now.

JL: The thing with Al-Quaeda is that it's become a thing because someone thought of the word. There is no Al-Quaeda network, well there is now, because people sign up to an idea, but that idea has been created.

JM: What does Al-Quaeda actually mean anyway?

IDLER: I don't know.

JM: It means "the righteous" or something [it means 'The Base', Ed]. It's like, Jihad doesn't actually mean anything like what we all think it means, but I've forgotten that too.

JL: In the Koran Jihad is the struggle to overcome oneself but it's misused to mean "kill other people".

JM: I didn't know the Koran was written in poetry. Instead of having the Gospels at the core of Christianty you would have Dante, or *Paradise Lost*.

JL: It's one of the good reasons to learn Arabic, of course, like learning Italian to read Dante. It makes it completely different to reading it in English.

JM: I did do that. I translated the whole of the *Inferno* when I was learning Italian at the same time. I had four months in Italy. But I'd come up with these Italian phrases which would be like Chaucerian phrases in modern Italian [laughs] ... because it's supposed to be the purist Italian. It was written about 500 years ago.

IDLER: So the success of the QI project, the books and everything, presumably that must all be cause for huge celebration?

JL: But all it means is that people consume it. It becomes part of the establishment.

JM: You don't know the effect it has, because we don't want it to be something you have to sign for, and pay a subscription fee, where you have to agree to these rules and conditions. That's one of the great problems of political movements. They say, "right, now you've got the same views as us you have to stop thinking." All you really want to do is hope that some part of the spirit in which you create the things you create, other people will take off and make their own stuff out of.

IDLER: You know those reviews on Amazon? They're usually illiterate and stupid, well the negative ones are anyway, [laughs], well, someone said about my book: "I don't agree with everything he says in this book but that's not the point, you have to go in and do your own thing." I thought that was a really nice reaction.

JM: My favourite review of *Animal Ignorance* so far is the one that goes "fabulous, fabu-lous, fabulous, fabulous, fabulous, fabulous book. Fabulous. The kind of book you want to read to your lover in bed after a heavy meal." That's fine. I can retire on that now.

IDLER: When you do get letters, what do they say?

JM: We sometimes get letters from people picking us up on facts, which is great. Sometimes you get slightly worrying letters like the one Sarah got, from the guy who is so obsessed with QI he's decided to dedicate the rest of his life to it ... well, we all live these ridiculously impoverished imaginative lives, and it's completely unnecessary. All you have to do is talk to someone, to open things up. Even in a village, you just to have cross the road, strike up a conversation and listen.

JL: It's encapsulated in the idea that there are no dull things, only dull ways of expressing them. The best professor in the University can be dull, and the supercilious little two year old.

IDLER: That was the precursor to all this, the "dullness" of the 18th century. They used the word bore to mean boring work, cant.

JM: It's the same, cant, but again it's people who don't reflect.

JL: There's no question that people must have had boring days and dull people but ...

JM: It's vanity, which actually means emptiness. If you read Ecclesiastes, "Vanity, vanity all is vanity" and you replace that with emptiness or boredom, it works. All those great Roman satirits, like Juvenal, always attacked that venal, empty ...

JL: We all, if we're honest, know the difference between an empty thing and something that somehow matters. You can do it in comedy. You can say "well, so and so, I suppose they're quite funny but there's no

The third most dangerous occupation in China is journalism.

meaning' and we do it with programmes. We say, that's a good programme because they matter in some way. It's very difficult to say, what's the meaning of meaning? That's why it's a pointlesss question to ask, "is the Universe meaningful?" because what does meaningful mean? But we *know*. It's another way of thinking. It's almost beyond intuition, you've tapped into something that you know is important, in some way, but you couldn't possibly say why.

JM: There's a great Wallace Stevens line which says "a meaning of a poem is another poem".

IDLER: But that doesn't mean you can't read critical essays about Blake or something.

JL: A good piece of literary criticism is about an insight, isn't it? It's a connection, what he's saying here is …

JM: It always amazes me that the slowest moving part of any bookshop is the section on literary criticism. It's misnamed. In our bookshop we called it essays.

JL: I don't know about essays. That's not good marketing. There should be a better word than that. There are a whole class of words that make you nod off, "education" is one. But I mean, what could be more interesting than teaching children?

JM: But as soon as you hear someone say "education" you know the conversation is dead.

JL: "Religion", "Environment", they're all the really important things …

IDLER: It's because they are co-opted. It's like "Health and Safety". It's been borified by Government.

JL: But hang on, there you go! "Health and Safety": what two more important things for human existence could there be? But we hate the very phrase!

IDLER: "Work and Pensions".

JL: Aarrggghhh!! Please, please, no more!

IDLER: I suppose if you had a "Department of Merriment in Everyday Life" it would become boring after a while.

JM: Merriment is fantastic.

JL: The Department of Merriment? I'd definitely go there. Imagine if they called the Department of Environment "The Department of Delicious Food".

IDLER: I don't know. I think it would quickly become very boring: "Oh no, I've got a Delicious Food meeting, bloody hell, not again …"

JM: Meetings should be banned.

IDLER: Meetings are quite fun when you're in them but when they're coming up …

JM: There should be a Liff for that, "sense of dread in anticipation of a meeting".

❖

JM: It's a very interesting thing though, who are you fighting against? Who is battle going to be joined against in the end?

IDLER: I think what you were saying that when you fight something you only make it stronger.

JL: Yep.

IDLER: So in QI you try not to kick against the things you oppose because that will strengthen them?

JM: But it's a society that also has no confidence at all. That's the whole thing that consumer society is about. Buying things simply to make people feel better about themselves. What's wonderful about what we do at QI, and I certainly believe it has a definite spiritual impact on you as a human being, is you work on stuff and you learn stuff, and it's free. All of it is free.

JL: That's it really. You don't need money to be interested. A little bit of money for a couple of bottles of wine is very cheap entertainment.

JM: I got a text from a friend of mine who's very funny, an alternative comedian, it said, "Jeremy Clarkson, Jimmy Carr, what next? Jonathan Ross? yours disappointedly." And you just think, Fuck off!

IDLER: What did he mean?

JM: There are certain hippies out there and Clarkson is their worst nightmare.

JL: Jimmy Carr and Jeremy Clarkson are much more interesting people than they're given credit for. And much more radical actually, and likeable.

IDLER: The people who slag off Jeremy Clarkson often hate him because they'd like to be like Jeremy Clarkson themselves.

JM: You've got to be a humourless twat not to find Top Gear funny. You've got to try really hard. My boys were watching one the other day where he'd done out the inside of a Mercedes as a country cottage with a log burning stove, rocking chairs and a wood floor and ornaments. It's a fantasy we've all had. He's just saying how shit the interior design of a car is. Then the other guy test drives it and the chimney falls off, and you can see people saying, "it's just childish".

IDLER: He just doesn't care.

JM: I'm very fond of George Monbiot, I've known him for ages, but come on.

IDLER: There's this horrifying thing from Jonathan Porrit who's saying "inaction, inaction, that's what's stopping everything!" But our green philosophy in the Idler is "action" is what's caused all the problems in the first place. Retreat, inaction is what's needed. Do less stuff.

JM: There is an amazing truth that when you do less more happens.

IDLER: I find that the more you disconnect from the media the clearer idea you get of what's going on.

JM: Newspapers are hysterical aren't they?

IDLER: I've got a very pompous idea for a book called the Nature of Things. Things have a nature, so for example email, by its nature, tends to make people communicate in a kind of rude fashion. And if you write a letter with a fountain pen then it will have a different nature to one written with a scratchy biro. And you can take this idea out further ...

JL: That's Plato's theories of forms, Tom,

IDLER: Is it?

JM: You're definitely right, it's like a difference between a hotpot and a frying pan. There's a determinism there.

IDLER: The heat from wood is different from heat that comes from gas or electricity.

JM: Those horrible fake glowing gas fires. This is going back to the point that there's this vast edifice of knowledge that's completely ignored. Of course we know a lot more now that they did in the past. I think we've probably forgotten at least as much. The stuff we've forgotten is the stuff we don't think is useful anymore, like what the wood from a beech tree is good for. Or planting by the moon, or whatever it is.

IDLER: It's very hubristic to think that we're at a point now where we know more than we've ever known before.

JM: Do you think we know more about raising children than we did 200 years ago?

IDLER: There is the argument that Rousseau, in Emile, was reacting against quite a brutal approach to childhood. And people read Philip Ariès who said that childhood

Work is a bigger killer than either drink or drugs, and is three times more dangerous than war.

didn't exist in the medieval age. But every medieval historian I've read completely slags that book off. Some of the most intelligent people I've been reading about recently never went to school.

JL: Really?

IDLER: John Stuart Mill didn't go to school. He was taught by Jeremy Bentham and his dad. Blake didn't go to school. I'm going to do a great list of these amazing people who never went to school. Bertrand Russell was another and it can tend to produce a more independent mind.

JM: Did you enjoy school, Tom?

IDLER: Yes.

JL: I hated it.

JM: Sometimes I wake up now and think, however bad it is, it won't be as bad as that feeling you have about exams.

IDLER: Now, what would a QI school look like?

JL: A QI school, well, there would be no work for a start, it would all be play. Plato said that education should be a form of amusement, that way you will be much better able to discover the child's natural bent. The first few years, until eight or nine, is just larking about having fun. Then you decide, well this child is musical, this one is artistic, this one is good at science, and you only educate children in the things they want to know about. And by the time these people are eleven or twelve they'll be University level but all the other stuff, the Geography, History, foreign languages and so on, that's just fun. That's all stories.

JM: Music, storytelling, doing stuff with your hands. That's how we interact with the world. There's that great line: you're taught for the first five years of your life to walk and talk, and for the next ten you're told to shut up and sit down. Kids figure things out so quickly when they want to. It's about trying to work with what's natural. And I know this.

JL: I must just tell you the story about this French Exchange student we had. He was the most polite little boy, he's not a child at all, he's really sixty years old. He comes from a very intellectual French family, and the Lloyds are all, "oh, yeah, well, whatever ..." After Sunday lunch, my wife Sarah had laid out all the Sunday papers, and she says: "would you like to sit by the fire and read the newspapers or go and play the Sims?" and he says, "I zink the Sims would be the more pleasant option."

JM: What I would say is that schools are really crap at harnessing the genius that kids have for screens and finding stuff. You shouldn't set it up as a battle, you should use it.

JL: If it was being done properly you wouldn't need to do that because you'd be talking, ferreting like John does [Mitchinson owns a ferret], or I play golf with Harry. He'd a million times rather go and play on the golf driving range than play a computer game, but maybe I'm not free, or tired or whatever. But there's no substitute for direct experience. But if you could find a way to use those computer games to teach people languages ... Harry's got this thing called "Medieval Castle" where you have to fight your way in, but if you just made that castle French, and you had to have French words to get past the guard, he'd be able to speak French in three weeks. This over here is just dissed as being stupid crap, while that over there is important because it's education, but education should be more interesting than computer games! And then we would not have any problems. Parents are all wankers though, aren't they? We're all shit at it. Well, not John.

IDLER: That's why I'm not against boarding schools in principle. My brother went at 13 and it was fantastic, he was free of his family.

JL: I think music should be part of a compulsory core curriculum as it was in Classical times and all the way through the Middle Ages. But music is taught in the most banal, tedious fucking way by most music teachers, which is "you will learn the basics, you will learn to read music, hands up like this, no that's wrong … No, that's a C not a D, you stupid little boy, why didn't you practise?" And Harry loves music, he always has, so I said, you're going to learn to play the piano, because you will so regret it if you don't. So for four years I ranted and screamed at him, and every practice he had when he was small he physically fought me, and screamed at me. And I have grade five theory in music, I can't play at all but I decided to pick out these pathetic tunes they have, "The Jolly Farmer". I practised these tunes, learned them by heart and played them to him. Within two plays he'd learned to play them. He couldn't read music, he's dyslexic, to him music on a page is Chinese. Harry went over to stay with the French exchange student. Harry likes hip hop and house but he also likes good rock music. And this 16-year-old French kid turned him on to Mozart, so now Harry's got an iPod full of Mozart. And as a result of that, this guy, who is a very good pianist, says to Harry, this is a good piece of Beethoven, easy to learn. Harry, who cannot read a fucking note of music, learned to play the piece note perfect in about an hour. He plays from

memory. But when I said to his prep school, "teach him some songs he cares about, teach him some Beatles songs," they said, "oh no, we can't do that because the Beatles never composed for piano." Paul McCartney never knew how to read music! They call it "learning difficulties" but it's learning differences. Harry doesn't want to learn the boring tedious stuff that the obedient kids are happy to be forcefed. I was one of the obedient ones, who said, "oh yeah, I get this really dull explanation of 18th century news politics. You really want me to repeat that to you?"

JM: So what is this perverse thing in parents that makes them want to make their kids suffer in the way they did at school? Out of some belief that it's going to help them? The other thing of course is tremendous guilt because of the economic imperative that so many parents feel for not being around for their kids because they have to work.

IDLER: I think a lot of it comes down to conditioning and brain washing.

JM: Well, it's collective madness.

IDLER: I think it's planned.

JL: Was it? It was certainly planned in the states Coolidge in 1907 had a big thing about education and what it was for, and they divided the country into two kinds. The intellectuals and then the ones needed to operate machinery who they deliberatley didn't want to have a high level of education because somebodies got to do the work.

IDLER: Huxley says in *Brave New World*: "we tried enslaving people against their will but that doesn't work. We've got to make them love their slavery." That's the key. And these things are planned. We all know how we have meetings about how we're going to

Anyone can do any amount of work, provided it isn't the work he is supposed to be doing at the moment. ROBERT BENCHLEY

market our books, how we're going to hopefully manipulate people's minds by getting them to buy our books. Governments do that as well. It's like after 9/11 and everyone had to go shopping. The creation of a consumer economy was a deliberate thing. We've got to keep producing, we've got to stimulate demand.

JM: When you say it's deliberate ... it's difficult to know whether it's just an aggregation of a lot of people over a period of time.

JL: I wonder if it's conscious. I mean every Christmas the newspapers say, "oh the high street shops have done really badly", but why are we supposed to care about Phillip Green? Why should we care whether Phillip Green's a million pounds less rich? It's not really explained. It's just "oh God, we better go out and buy more things," I think we are being manipulated.

JM: When you listen to Gordon Brown, all he ever talks about is "not wanting to be left behind". It's how somehow, if we don't have enough skilled people we'll be left behind in the global thing.

IDLER: An interviewer complained to me when I praised idling: "But we've got to be competitive!"

JM: But what does that mean? It's like fear of the sky falling in. It seems to me that you're competitive as a country if you've got good ideas. The whole country though, what are we talking about? The idea that living on an estate in Newcastle gives you any sense of kinship with the rest of the country ...

IDLER: Queen Victoria's Coronation was an attempt to get some patriotic spirit going, but before that people in the countryside barely knew who she was. These things are deliberately done. Like the show at Crystal Palace, they'll be a public holiday so people can go and visit the great show and feel as though they are contributing to the commercial greatness of their country. It's propaganda. I think everyone underestimates how much we are manipulated all the time. We can believe it of 100 years ago or even twenty years ago, but we don't seem to believe it's happening now.

JM: So we're all complicit in the end. One of the curious things now is there is nowhere you can go and be outside the market. There was a fantasy for a while that you could go to the Eastern bloc, but actually that was all nonsense.

IDLER: What was it like on your trip to the South Seas, Mitch?

JM: Raratonga? I think the problem is that what you discover in those traditional societies, have you ever watched *Tribe* on TV? They are extraordinarily good shows. Well Bruce Parry, the presenter, did a thing on the Island of Anuta where they have a concept called *Aropa*, or sharing. They have to share everything. It's a small island in the middle of nowhere. There's no consistency as to when the boats come, but some of them have now got money. And that's the one thing they don't share. They sell stuff and they get cash and that is causing tensions in their society. At the same time they can't decide whether they should have a clinic on the island. The chief is saying, "if you bring in a clinic it will undermine the old ways." It's hard not to see that the triumph of Western culture is like a virus. It does kind of corrupt everything it touches but at the same time it would be naïve and dishonest not to say that it is compelling. There is something compelling about it.

IDLER: New markets. That's the William

Morris thing. They had all these same issues in 1890.

JM: But we're all complicit.

JL: There's so much information in the QI database, which is my name for all the things I have learned for myself. A very long list. Hundreds and hundreds of pages on everything from chemical elements to French botanists and ...

Isotope, do you know what an isotope is? Try and look up on the Internet to find an explanation that is satisfying for you and there's no such place. On the QI database you'll find a very simple and easy to understand definition. At the moment it's been the damnedest struggle just staying alive, keeping afloat and solvent, in the last few years. But one day we think this is going to be the new Google, Wikipedia. I mean Wikipedia is great. I use it all the time, but it's wobbly quality.

JM: It's a refreshing fountain you can go to.

JL: It tells you where the treasure is buried. It definitely does.

JM: *The Companion to English Literature*. It's shocking that the book about perhaps the most interesting thing in the world, all the greatest writers, I mean you can read the whole of that book and not remember a single things afterwards. How can you make Dickens dull?

JL: Who are the famous Victorian historians, MacCauley, Gibbon? Well, one of the facts on the QI database is that in the *Encyclopedia Britannica* entry on Edward Gibbon there is not one single interesting thing in the biography entry and he had the most fascinating life. You've really got to dig.

JM: Gibbons were named after him.

JL: No! That is so good.

JM: It's better than that. The guy who first described them was Gibbon's best friend and there are two arguments, one was that they were called "Gib" because they looked like cats or Gibbons because of his best mate. What are you going to call a new monkey when you haven't got a name for them?

JL: That is so brilliant. Now I don't understand how I lived, Tom, how I got through a week without having this sort of conversation. That's the wonderful thing about QI. It does you good when you hear that.

JM: Some deep electrical thing happens. Humour, interestingness and sexual attraction, they're all ... it is electrical. You know if you could see your brain the moment those little connections are made, "yippee".

JL: One of the funniest things I ever heard on the *News Quiz* was this news cutting about this cleaner who'd been sacked from his job because he'd spent all day cleaning the elevator because he thought it was a different one on each floor. Why is that so funny? It's like John says, humour's about connection.

The work will teach you how to do it. ESTONIAN PROVERB

QI QUESTIONS

*Sixteen Curiosities from
the QI Vaults*

1. What drives human sperm wild?

The smell of Lily of the Valley.

It appears sperm have "noses" which they use to navigate towards a woman's egg. Researchers experimented with a range of floral fragrances and Lily of the Valley came top, getting the random sperm wiggling in the same direction at twice the normal speed.

The research was carried out at Ruhr University in Germany in 2003. They discovered a new sperm protein, hOR174, which acted as a receptor for sperm in exactly the same way as protein sensors in the nose detect smells. They then tested their new sperm "nose" on hundreds of synthetic compounds, many of them used to mimic floral scents in commercial perfumes.

One of these, bourgeonal, is used to create the Lily of the Valley fragrance. It had two dramatic effects on the behavior of sperm: doubling its speed and changing undirected swimming behavior to direct movement. The "foot-to-the-floor" effect seems to derive from hOR17-4 making the sperm wag their "tails" harder.

Bourgeonal is now being used in fertility treatment to pick out the Mark Spitzes of the sperm world.

2. Why was the dishwasher invented?

Not to make doing the dishes easier.

Its main purpose was to reduce the number of breakages caused by servants, rather than to act as a labor-saving device.

The first practical mechanical dishwasher was invented in 1886 by Josephine Garis Cochran (1839–1913) of Shelbyville, Illinois. She was the daughter of a civil engineer and, on her mother's side, the great-grand-daughter of John "Crazy" Fitch, the inventor of the steamboat. A prominent socialite, married to a merchant and politician, her main problem in life was worrying about the maids chipping her precious china (it had been in the family since the 17th century).

This enraged her and, so the story goes, one night she dismissed the servants, did the dishes on her own, saw what an impossible job it was and vowed, if no one else would, to invent a machine to do it instead. When her husband William died in 1883, leaving her in debt, she got serious.

With the help of an engineer friend, she designed the machine in her woodshed. It was crude and cumbersome but effective. There was a small foot-pedal driven version and a large steam-driven one. The latter, able to wash and dry 200 dishes in two minutes, was the sensation of the 1893 Chicago World's Fair, and won first prize for the "best mechanical construction for durability and adaptation to its line of work". At $250 each, however, the machines were too expensive for home use, but enough were sold to hotels and restaurants to keep *Cochran's Crescent Washing Machine Company* in business until her death in 1913.

Other mechanical dishwashers had been developed (and patented) in the U.S. between 1850 and 1865 (all of them, it seems, by women) but none of them really worked. A hand cranked wooden machine was invented and patented in 1850 by Joel Houghton. In 1870, Mary Hobson obtained a dishwasher patent, but even then it contained the word "improved". The electric dishwasher first appeared in 1912; the first specialised dishwasher detergent (Calgon) in 1932; the first automatic dishwasher in 1940, but it didn't reach Europe until 1960.

❖

Housework can kill you, if you do it right.
ERMA BOMBECK

3. What's a *vomitorium* for?

Vomitorium, despite being derived from the Latin *vomere*, meaing "to spew forth" isn't the place where the Romans threw up after their meals. It was the name for the entrance or exit from an amphitheatre and is still used in that sense today in some sports stadiums.

The *vomitoria* of the Colosseum in Rome were so well designed that it's said the venue, which seated at least 50,000, could fill in 15 minutes. (There were 80 entrances at ground level, 76 for ordinary spectators and 4 for the imperial family.)

The confusion of the exit with a specialised vomit chamber appears to be a recent error. The earliest citation in the *Oxford English Dictionary* finds Aldous Huxley using the term incorrectly in his 1923 comic novel, *Antic Hay*, with the stern comment "erron." Lewis Mumford in *The City in History* (1961) compounded the confusion by saying the exits were named after the chambers where gluttons threw up "in order to return to their couches empty enough to enjoy the pleasures of still more food."

The problem with this theory is that no Roman writer ever refers to them, nor have any purpose-built rooms that fit the bill been found. Romans certainly threw up on purpose. Indeed, in ancient times vomiting seems to have been a standard part of the fine-dining experience. The orator Cicero, in *Pro Rege Deiotaro* (45 B.C.), says that Julius Caesar "expressed a desire to vomit after dinner" and elsewhere suggests that the dictator took emetics for this purpose.

But where did they do it, if there was no special room? Some sources suggest the street or garden; others are adamant it was at the table. In his *Moral Epistles* the Roman philosopher Seneca writes: "When we recline at a banquet, one slave wipes up the spittle; another, situated beneath the table, collects the leavings of the drunks."

In another passage, in a letter to his mother Helvia he links this to the decadent pursuit of the new and the exotic: "they vomit that they may eat, they eat that they may vomit, and they do not deign even to digest the feasts for which they ransack the whole world."

4. What did Robert Bunsen invent?

Many things, but not the Bunsen Burner.

Robert Wilhelm Bunsen (1811–1899) was an influential German chemist and teacher who devised or improved the design of a number of pieces of laboratory equipment still in use today. However, the item he is most famous for was actually invented by the English chemist Michael Faraday and then improved by Peter Desaga, Bunsen's technician at the University of Heidelberg,

Bunsen first became renowned in the scientific community for his work on arsenic. He eventually discovered the only known antidote to the poison, but not before losing his sight in one eye and almost dying of arsenic poisoning.

He went on to produce a galvanic battery that used a carbon element instead of the much more expensive platinum. Using this he was able to isolate pure chromium, magnesium, aluminum, and other metals. At the same time, he also solved the riddle of how geysers worked by building a working model in his lab.

The need for a new style of burner grew out of his work with a young physicist called Gustav Kirchoff. Together they pioneered the technique that became known as spectroscopy. By filtering light through a prism they discovered that every element had its own signature spectrum. In order to produce this light by heating different materials, they needed a flame that was very hot but not very bright.

Bunsen developed this new heat source using Faraday's burner as his starting point. In the earlier model, the oxygen was added at the point of combustion, which led to a smoky, flickery flame. Bunsen conceived a burner where oxygen was mixed with gas before combustion in order to make a very hot, blue flame. He took his ideas to Desaga, who built the prototype in 1855.

Within five years, Bunsen and Kirchoff had used the combination of their new burner and sceptroscope to identify the elements caesium and rubidium. Their lab became famous, and Bunsen's modesty and eccentricity (he never washed) brought him international renown. Mendeleyev, the Russian inventor of the periodic table, was one of his many devoted pupils.

Although he didn't get to give his name to the burner he built, Desaga did get the rights to sell it, which his family did very successfully (and profitably) for several generations.

Despite its iconic status, the Bunsen burner has now largely been replaced in chemistry labs by the cleaner and safer electric hot plate.

5. What happens if you cut an earthworm in half?

You get two halves of a dead worm, usually. Sometimes the head end survives, but you can't get two worms from one.

Some species of worm can regenerate amputated tails, depending on how many body segments they've lost, and some species jettison tails to escape predators, but the headless part will always die, as will the head if it hasn't retained sufficient body. The death throes of the severed sections can go on for hours, and could easily be mistaken for lively wriggling.

The "both ends become a worm" idea seems to have started as a way of shutting up small children. Sadly, nobody ever gets round to telling you that it isn't true once you've grown up.

The smooth band a third of the way along an earthworm isn't the "join" from which the "new worm" grows. It is called the *clitellum* and is responsible for secreting the sticky clear mucus that covers the worm.

There is a freshwater flatworm called a *planaria* or "cross-eyed worm" which also has an extraordinary ability to regenerate itself when damaged. The American geneticist and Nobel laureate T.H. Morgan (1866–1945) found that a piece of planaria 1/279th of its original size could regenerate into a full-sized planaria, and a planaria split lengthwise *or* crosswise will regenerate into two separate individuals.

6. What rhymes with orange?

There are two rhymes for orange in English, although both are proper nouns: Blorenge and Gorringe.

The Blorenge is a hill outside Abergavenny in Wales, and Gorringe is a splendid English surname

The best view of Abergavenny is from the top of the Blorenge, a 1,833 ft hill owned by the South East Wales Hang-gliding and Paragliding Club, who bought it from the Coal Authority in 1998.

Distinguished Gorringes include: General George Frederick Gorringe (1865–1945), the unpopular British First World War commander; Harry Gorringe, the first-class Australian cricketer; and Henry Honeychurch Gorringe, the man who brought Cleopatra's Needle from Egypt to New York's Central Park.

In 1673, New York was called New Orange (so the New Orange became the Big Apple). The city was founded by the Dutch in 1653 as New Amsterdam, taken by the English in 1664 and renamed New York, and retaken by the Dutch in 1673 and named New Orange. It lasted less than a year. Under the Treaty of Westminster in 1674 the city was ceded to the English, and New York became its permanent name.

The word "orange" is a good example of what linguists call wrong word division. It derives from the Arabic *naranj* and arrived in English as "narange" in the 14th century, gradually losing the initial "n". The same process left us with apron (from *naperon*) and umpire (from *noumpere*).

Sometimes it works the other way round, as in nickname (from an *eke-name*, meaning "also-name") or newt (from an *ewt*).

Orange was first used as the name for a colour in 1542.

7. What's interesting about the birth of Julius Caesar?

Almost nothing is known about the birth of Julius Caesar, except that, contrary to the assertion in the *Oxford English Dictionary* and countless other reference books, it did not take place by Caesarean section.

Such operations did occur at the time, but they always involved the death of the mother, and Caesar's mother Aurelia is known to have survived into his adulthood. The suggestion that he was born by C-section does not appear in any of the contemporary sources, and is first mentioned in medieval times. It is first used in a medical context in English in 1615.

The confusion probably started with Pliny the Elder who, in his *Natural History* (ca. 77 A.D.) claims that the first Caesar was "cut from his mother's womb". This may well have been true, but it wasn't the Caesar we know as Gaius Julius Caesar. The Roman three-part naming convention meant that Gaius was his "given name" and he was part of the "Caesar" branch of the "Julian" clan, so no one knows how many Caesars there had been previously. Nor do we know exactly what "Caesar" means — and none of the meanings are particularly apt to our man. There is Pliny's "cut" from *caedere*. Or *caeseries* meaning "hairy" (but he was balding); or *caesius* "grey" (but his eyes were black) or even "elephant" (from the Phoenician and perhaps applied to an Julian ancestor who had killed one).

The Roman's pronounced "Caesar" as *kaiser* (which is still the German word for King and, like the Russian *czar,* ultimately derived from Caesar). All the Roman emperors after Julius, and until Hadrian, were called "Caesar".

Caesar Salad is no relation, however. It was invented by Cesar Cardini in an Italian restaurant in Tijuana, Mexico in 1923.

8. How did Mark Twain get his name?

He stole it.

The usual explanation is that he took the name from the call of the leadsman on a Mississippi paddle boat steamer. "Mark Twain" was the second mark on the lead-line used to calculate the river's depth. It indicated a depth of 2 fathoms (12 feet), which was "safe water".

This isn't wrong, it's just that someone else had got there first. The name was already being used by Captain Isaiah Sellers (1802–1863), the river news correspondent for the *New Orleans Picayune*.

The young Samuel Longhorn Clemens (1835–1910) cut his teeth writing parodies of Sellers under the pen name Sergeant Fathom. According to Clemens, Sellers was "not of a literary turn or capacity" but was "a fine man, a high-minded man, and greatly respected both ashore and on land". The Sergeant Fathom burlesques mortified him. Clemens later wrote: "He had never been held up to ridicule before; he was sensitive, and he never got over the hurt which I had wantonly and stupidly inflicted upon his dignity."

This didn't stop stealing his pen name, as Twain (Mark II) explained in a letter to a reader:

> Dear Sir,
> 'Mark Twain' was the *nom de plume* of one Capt. Isaiah Sellers, who used to write river news over it for the *New Orleans Picayune*. He died in 1863, and as he could no longer need that signature, I laid violent hands upon it without asking permission of the proprietor's remains. That is the history of the *nom de plume* I bear.
> Yours truly,
> Samuel L. Clemens

9. Whose official motto is *e pluribus unum*?

E pluribus unum ('out of the many, one') is the motto of the Portuguese football club *Sport Lisboa e Benfica* — usually abbreviated to Benfica.

E Pluribus Unum used to be the national motto of the United States, referring to the integration of the 13 founding states (it has thirteen letters), but it was replaced by "In God we trust" (a line from 'The Star-Spangled Banner') as the official national motto in 1956. The confusion arises because *e pluribus unum* is still used in the Great Seal, on the ribbon streaming from the eagle's mouth, which appears on the reverse of the dollar bill and on all U.S. coins.

The phrase was originally used to describe a herby cheese spread. In a Latin recipe poem called *Moretum,* once attributed to Virgil, the poet describes the lunch of a simple farmer in which he grinds cheese, garlic and herbs together into a ball (*color est e pluribus unus*). By the 18th century it had become a well-worn phrase meaning unity or friendship.

Benfica was created as a merger of two clubs in 1908. It is Portugal's most popular soccer club, but also fields teams in a range of other sports as well.

10. In what year did World War II end?

In 1990.

Although actual hostilities came to an end with the Japanese surrender signed on September 2, 1945, the Cold War got in the way of a formal legal settlement. Peace treaties were signed with Italy, Romania, Hungary, Bulgaria, and Finland in 1950. All the Allies except the U.S.S.R. signed a treaty with Japan in 1951. Austria waited until 1955 to regain its sovereignty. Germany, however, was divided between the Western powers and the U.S.S.R., and no peace treaty was signed with what emerged as the German Democratic Republic in 1949.

So, the first celebration of German reunification, on October 3, 1990, marks the official end to World War II.

The United States has formally declared war just 11 times: twice against Germany, twice against Hungary (1917, in its guise as Austria-Hungary, and 1942) and once each against Romania (1942), Bulgaria (1942), Italy (1941), Japan (1941), Spain (1898), Mexico (1898) and the United Kingdom (1812).

The Vietnam War and the two Iraq campaigns were not formal declarations of war, but "military engagements authorized by Congress". Under the 1973 War Powers Act, the President gained authority to deploy troops (within certain limits of size and time) without a formal declaration. Formal declarations are disliked because they lend legitimacy to unrecognised or unpopular regimes.

The Korean War was neither formally declared nor approved by Congress and despite hostilities ending in 1953, a peace treaty has never been signed with North Korea.

The longest war fought by the United States was the forty-six year campaign against the Apache nation which ended in 1886 with Geronimo's surrender at Skeleton Canyon, New Mexico.

War is God's way of teaching Americans geography.

AMBROSE BIERCE

❖

11. Is a virus a germ?

Yes, "germ" is an informal term for any biological agent that causes illness to its host and so covers both viruses and bacteria.

Viruses and bacteria are quite different. Viruses are microscopic parasites too small to have cells or even their own metabolism. Their growth is entirely dependent on their host. Each infected host cell becomes a virus factory capable of producing thousands of copies of the invading virus. The common cold, small-pox and herpes are viral infections and can be treated by vaccination but not antibiotics.

Bacteria are simple but cellular, the most abundant of all organisms. There are approximately 10,000 species living in or on the human body: a healthy human will be carrying ten times as many bacterial cells as human cells, and they account for about 10 percent of dry body weight. The vast majority are benign, and many are beneficial. Bacterial illnesses include tetanus, typhoid fever, pneumonia, syphilis, cholera, food poisoning, leprosy, and tuberculosis and they are treatable with antibiotics.

The word "germ" comes from the Latin *germen* meaning "sprout" or "bud". It was first used to describe a harmful micro-organism in 1871 and it wasn't until 1875 that Robert Koch finally demonstrated that anthrax was caused by a particular species of bacteria.

Thirty-five years earlier, Ignaz Semmelweis, a Hungarian doctor had set up the first hygienic hospital ward in Vienna General Hospital. He noticed that the death rate of poor women attended by the nurse midwives was three times less than that of the wealthier women attended by the doctors. He concluded that this was a matter of cleanliness — the doctors used to go directly from the morgue to the obstetrics ward without washing their hands. When he presented his findings, his fellow doctors rejected his theory, unable to believe in what they could not see.

In recent years, however, hygiene itself has come under scrutiny. There does seem to be evidence that indiscriminate use of anti-bacterial agents might have damaging side effects, allowing those bacteria that do survive to mutate into even more virulent strains. Also, our immune system, deprived of bacteria and parasites that it has struggled against for thousands of years, has a tendency to overreact leading to a sharp upswing in allergic diseases such asthma, diabetes and rheumatoid arthritis.

Despite this, infectious diseases still kill more people than anything else and 80% of those diseases are transmitted by touch.

Most hygienists recommend that washing our hands regularly with good old-fashioned soap and water is the best and safest way to stay healthy.

12. Where does the equals sign come from?

Wales.

This essential constituent of mathematics wasn't a product of the Greeks, the Babylonians or the Arabs, but the small coastal town of Tenby in South Wales. There, in 1510, the astronomer and mathematician Robert Recorde was born. Recorde was a child prodigy who rose to prominence as Royal physician to Edward VI and Queen Mary, and later as controller of the Royal Mint.

He was also a prolific author, writing a sequence of popular maths textbooks, of which *The Whetstone of Witte* (1557) is the most famous. Not only did it introduce algebra to an English audience for the first time it also introduced the equals sign =.

Recorde's reason for adopting two parallel lines is refreshingly to the point: "bicause noe 2 thynges, can be moare equalle." It took a while to catch on: || and *ae* (from "aequalis") were used well into the 17th century.

One Recorde invention which didn't stick was his word describing numbers to the eighth power, e.g. $2^8 = 256$. *Zenzizenzizenzic* was based on the German *zenzic*, a version of the Italian *censo* meaning "squared" (so, it means "*x* squared, squared and squared again"). It does, however, comfortably hold the record for the number of zs in a single word.

Despite his facility with numbers Recorde was less good with his personal finances. Poor political judgment meant he got on the wrong side of the Earl of Pembroke who called in a debt for the then astronomical sum of £1,000. This broke Recorde and he died in the King's Bench debtors prison in Southwark, aged 48.

13. What are you doing when you "do the Hokey Pokey"?

You may be performing a sinister parody of the Roman Catholic Latin mass.

The theory goes that in the days when the priest celebrated the Mass facing the altar the congregation mimicked his gestures and the words as they misheard them behind his back. Thus the words "hokey pokey" are a corruption of the Latin phrase: *Hoc est enim corpus meum* ("This is my body").

It may also be related to "hocus pocus", the old conjuror's phrase dating from the early 17th century. By the end of the 18th century this had been contracted to make a new word, "hoax".

Whatever the origin, "hokey-pokey" came to mean "nonsense" and attached itself to early ice-cream street vendors who sold it as "Hokey-pokey penny a lump". Ice cream with toffee in it is still called Hokey-pokey in New Zealand and Australia.

In Britain, a dance with lyrics called "The Cokey Cokey", was copyrighted in 1942 by Jimmy Kennedy of "Teddy Bears' Picnic" fame. It seems to have been appropriated by a G.I. called Larry Laprise (a.k.a. "The Hokey Pokey Man") who carried it back to the U.S. were he and two friends adapted it for the *après-ski* crowd at a nightclub in Sun Valley, Idaho. His group, the Ram Trio, recorded the song as "The Hokey Pokey" in 1949 and it became a dance floor favorite.

Kennedy always claimed it his version was based on a traditional Canadian folk song, but it also seems to bear a striking resemblance to a Shaker song from Kentucky called "The Hinkum-Booby": *I put my right hand in, I put my right hand out, I give my right hand a shake, And I turn it all about.*

Whoever wrote it, and despite its possible religious (or Satanic) resonances, the dance has received become a firm favorite with foreign language teachers trying to get students to remember the names of their body parts in other languages.

Enoch, Methuselah's father, who's still alive. He's 5,387 years old, give or take a week. Methuselah lived to a measly 969.

Methuselah is famous for being the oldest man who ever lived but, according to the Bible, he was not that much older than his own grandfather, Jared, who lived to be 962. The direct line of Adam's descendants up until the Flood (with their ages) is as follows: Adam (930); Seth (912); Enos (905); Cainan (910); Mahalaleel (895); Jared (962); Enoch (365 not out); Methuselah (969); Lamech (777); Noah (950).

Though all of these characters were abnormally old, all but one of them died in a perfectly normal way. The exception is the mysterious Enoch, who was a stripling of just 365 when God "took him". Enoch never died at all: a distinction not even granted to Jesus Christ. In the New Testament. St Paul reiterates the story of Enoch's immortality in his Epistle to the Hebrews.

> *By faith Enoch was translated that he should not see death; and was not found, because God had translated him: for before his translation he had this testimony, that he pleased God.* (Hebrews 11:5)

The French philosopher Descartes believed it ought to be possible for all human beings to live as long as the Biblical Patriarchs — around 1,000 years — and was convinced he was on the brink of cracking the secret when he died in 1650, aged 54.

❖

My doctor told me that jogging could add years to my life.
I think he was right. I feel ten years older already.
MILTON BERLE

❖

15. Where does the word "assassin" come from?

Not from hashish.

The earliest authority for the medieval sect called the Assassins taking hashish in order to witness the pleasures awaiting them after death is the notoriously unreliable Marco Polo. Most Islamic scholars now favour the more convincing etymology of *assassiyun*, meaning people who are faithful to the *assass*, the "foundation" of the faith. They were, literally, "fundamentalists".

This makes sense when you look at their core activities. The Al-Hashishin, or Nizaris as they called themselves, were active for 200 years. They were Shi'ite muslims, dedicated to the overthrow of the Sunni Caliph (a kind of Islamic king). The Assassins considered the Baghdad regime decadent and little more than a puppet regime of the Turks. Sound familiar?

The sect was founded by Hassan-i Saban in 1090, a mystic philosopher, fond of poetry and science. They made their base at Alamut, an unassailable fortress in the mountains south of the Caspian Sea. It housed an important library and beautiful gardens but it was Hasan's political strategy that made the sect famous. He decided they could wield huge influence by using a simple weapon: terror.

Dressed as merchants and holy men they selected and murdered their victims in public, usually at Friday prayers, *in* the mosque. They weren't explicitly "suicide" missions, but the assassins were usually killed in the course of their work.

They were incredibly successful, systematically wiping out all the major leaders of the Muslim world and effectively destroying all chances of a unified Islamic defense against the Western crusaders.

What finally defeated them was, ironically, exactly what defeated their opponents. In 1256 Hulagu Khan assembled the largest Mongol army ever known. They marched westward destroying the assassins' power base in Alamut, before sacking Baghdad in 1258.

Baghdad was then the world's most beautiful and civilized city. A million citizens perished and so many books were thrown into the river Tigris it ran black with ink. The city remained a ruin for hundreds of years afterwards.

Hulagu destroyed the caliphs and the assassins. He drove Islam into Egypt and then returned home only to perish, in true Mongol style, in a civil war.

16. Where do kilts, bagpipes, haggis, porridge, whisky and tartan come from?

Not from Scotland.

In fact, not even "Scotland" is Scottish. Scotland is named after the *Scoti*, a Celtic tribe from Ireland, who arrived in what the Romans called Caledonia in the fifth or sixth century A.D. By the 11th century they dominated the whole of mainland Scotland. "Scots Gaelic" is actually a dialect of Irish.

Kilts were invented by the Irish but word "kilt" is Danish (*kilte op*, "tuck up").

The bagpipes are ancient and were probably invented in Central Asia. They are mentioned in the Old Testament (Daniel 3:5, 10, 15) and in Greek poetry of the 4th century B.C. The Romans probably brought them to Britain but the earliest Pictish carvings date from the 8th century A.D.

Haggis was an Ancient Greek sausage (Aristophanes mentions one exploding in *The Clouds* in 423 B.C.).

Oat porridge has been found in the stomachs of 5,000 year old Neolithic bog bodies in central Europe and Scandinavia.

Whisky was invented in ancient China. It arrived in Ireland before Scotland, first distilled by monks. The word derives from the Irish *uisge beatha*, from the Latin *aqua vitae* or "water of life".

The elaborate system of clan tartans is a complete myth stemming from the early nineteenth century. All Highland dress, including what tartan or plaid there was, was banned after the 1745 rebellion. The English garrison regiments started designing their own tartans as an affectation, and to mark the state visit of King George IV to Edinburgh in 1822. Queen Victoria encouraged the trend, and it soon became a Victorian craze.

Having said a' that, they've nae been idle, ye ken. Scots inventions and discoveries include: adhesive stamps; the Bank of England; bicycle pedals; the Breechloading rifle; Bovril; the cell nucleus; chloroform; the cloud chamber; colour photography; cornflour; the cure for malaria; the decimal point; the *Encyclopaedia Britannica*; electro-magnetism; the fountain pen; finger-printing; hypnosis; hypodermic syringes; insulin; kaleidoscopes; the Kelvin scale; the lawnmower; lime cordial; logarithms; lorries; marmalade; motor insurance; the MRI scanner; the paddle steamer; paraffin; piano pedals; the postmark; pneumatic tires; radar; the reflecting telescope; savings banks; the screw propeller; the speedometer; the steam hammer; the raincoat; tarmac; the teleprinter; tubular steel; the typhoid vaccine; the ultrasound scanner; the United States Navy; Universal Standard Time; vacuum flasks; wave-powered electricity generators, and wire rope. 🔊

ESSAYS

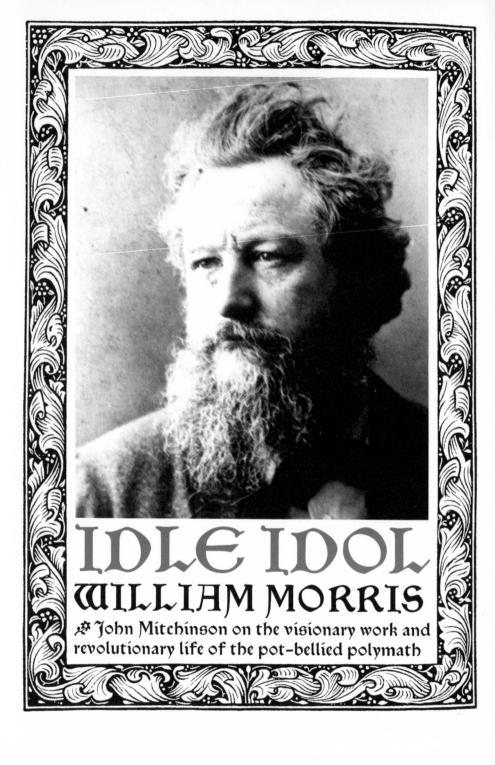

IDLE IDOL
WILLIAM MORRIS

John Mitchinson on the visionary work and
revolutionary life of the pot-bellied polymath

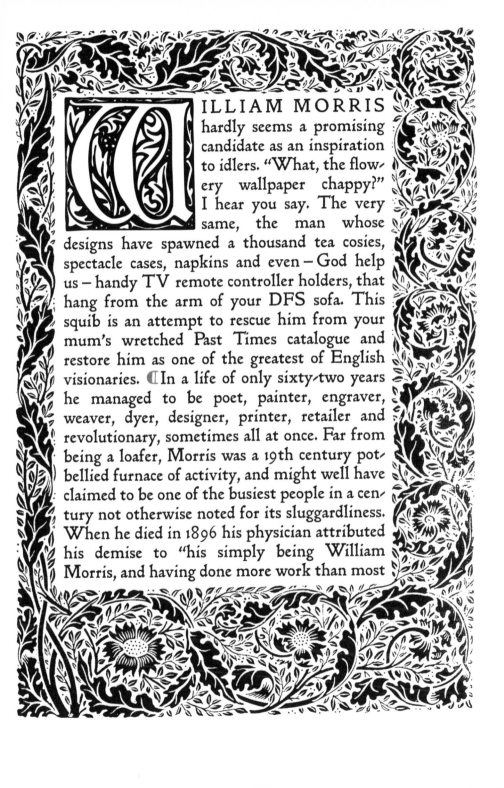

WILLIAM MORRIS hardly seems a promising candidate as an inspiration to idlers. "What, the flowery wallpaper chappy?" I hear you say. The very same, the man whose designs have spawned a thousand tea cosies, spectacle cases, napkins and even – God help us – handy TV remote controller holders, that hang from the arm of your DFS sofa. This squib is an attempt to rescue him from your mum's wretched Past Times catalogue and restore him as one of the greatest of English visionaries. ❡In a life of only sixty-two years he managed to be poet, painter, engraver, weaver, dyer, designer, printer, retailer and revolutionary, sometimes all at once. Far from being a loafer, Morris was a 19th century pot-bellied furnace of activity, and might well have claimed to be one of the busiest people in a century not otherwise noted for its sluggardliness. When he died in 1896 his physician attributed his demise to "his simply being William Morris, and having done more work than most ten men." So, what can such a compulsive over-achiever with a nice line in chintz offer as inspiration for those of us concerned with dropping out, down-shifting and kicking our tawdry, dull culture into touch? Quite a lot, as it turns out.

RUE IDLERS, of course, aren't lazy; they just work differently. Morris under-stood this instinctively. To him, all useful work (which he distinguished from "use less toil") was really a form of play:

> I think that to all living things there is a pleasure in the exercise of their energies, and that even beasts rejoice in being lithe and swift and strong. But a man at work, making something which he feels will exist because he is working at it and wills it, is exer-cising the energies of his mind and soul as well as of his body. Memory and imagination help him as he works. Not only his own thoughts, but the thoughts of the men of past ages guide his hands; and, as a part of the human race, he creates. If we work thus we shall be men, and our days will be happy and eventful.

❡ Work that satisfies and ennobles is hardly a new idea. Confucius said much the same thing 2,500 years earlier ("choose a job you love and you'll never have to work again") but few have articulated as thor-oughly or lived it as completely as Morris.
❡ He was born into a reasonably well-off family. His father was a city broker who died young, but shares in a Devon copper mine ensured the family enjoyed a

90

comfortable life. A certain guilt at this haunted Morris throughout his life, and he was endlessly generous to his friends as a result, entertaining royally and bank-rolling all their artistic joint-ventures. It also left him with a class-defying recklessness which is one of the many reasons he's still so much fun to read: "How often it consoles me to think of barbarism once more flooding the world and real feelings and passions, however, rudimentary, taking the place of our hypocrisies." In a letter to a friend he writes: "I am a boor and the son of a boor". You don't get much of this cocksure honesty in the high-flown prose of his Victorian contemporaries.

❡Morris's "dog-at-broth" quality could make him both lovable and exasperating. Edward Burne-Jones, the Pre-Raphaelite painter, and Morris's closest friend, catches the roller-coaster nature of Morris's life perfectly:

When I first knew Morris nothing would content him but being a monk, and getting to Rome, and then he must be an architect, and apprenticed himself to Street [the Gothic revival architect], and worked for two years, but when I came to London and began to paint he threw it all up, and must paint too, and then he must give it up and make poems, and then he must give it up and make window hangings and pretty things, and when he had achieved that, he must be a poet again, and then after two or three years of Earthly Paradise time, he must learn dyeing, and lived in a vat, and learned weaving, and knew all about looms, and then made more books, and learned tapestry, and then wanted to smash everything up and begin the world anew, and now it is printing he cares for, and to make wonderful rich-looking books – and all things he does splendidly – and if he lives the printing will have an end ... then he'll do I don't know what, but every minute will be alive.

❧ "Alive" is the key to Morris. He never felt more alive than when he was making something, and his enthusiasm and energy seemed to rub off on those around him. Whether at home, or in his factories and shops, Morris had a genius for getting other people to join in. Some of this was no doubt due to his eccentric charm. At Oxford he was noted for his purple trousers and once ate dinner in a suit of chain mail he'd commissioned from a local blacksmith. His friends called him Topsy (inspired by his unruly mop of hair and borrowed from the popular contemporary novel, Uncle Tom's Cabin) and through most of his working life he was a short, portly, barrel-chested, bright-eyed and untidy ball of energy, absent-minded, continually breaking chairs by what "Ned" Burne-Jones called "a muscular movement peculiar to himself" and capable of terrifying fits of foul-mouthed temper. When in a rage, Topsy could crush forks with his teeth, smash holes in plaster walls with his head and once threw an undercooked plum pudding through a window on Christmas Day. In return, his friends would wind him up terribly, moving his waistcoat buttons to make him feel even more fat, or refusing to answer his questions at dinner. Sometimes – as in the case of Dante Gabriel Rossetti, who was his wife Janey's lover for almost twenty years – this teasing became cruel (Rossetti named his pet wombat Tops after him) but mostly it was with Morris's enthusiastic compliance. He liked being the centre of attention, even when it cast him in an absurd light. He was a man of great appetites: he "lusted for pig's flesh" and always kept the dinner table groaning with good wine ("Why do people say it is so prosaic to be inspired by wine. Has it not been made by the sunlight and the sap?") He liked the grand gesture, sitting on his top hat to mark his resignation from the board of his family's copper mine when he became a socialist. With his shaggy beard, blue work shirt and rolling gait, he was often mistaken, to his delight, for a seaman, and there are times when he does seem like a Viking that has stepped out of one of his beloved Norse sagas.

⁋ Despite being a bit of nutter, this Morris still sounds like someone you'd like to spend an evening with in the pub. He was lovable, naughty, unforgettable. And, sure enough, wherever you look, Morris fans appear, like birds hidden in one of his matchless tapestries. The young Rudyard Kipling rembered his "Uncle Topsy" telling wonderful, if rather macabre, bedtime stories. W.B. Yeats – not known for his generosity to fellow writers – adored Morris and wrote: "If some angel offered me the choice, I would choose to live his life, poetry and all, rather than any other man's." Henry James found him "very agreeable". "He is short, burly, corpulent, very careless and unfinished in his dress … His talk indeed is wonderfully to the point and remarkable for dear, good sense." He has been called the father of Modernism in architecture (Niklaus Pevsner), the most important English socialist thinker (E.P. Thompson) and the Greens claim him as our first Environmentalist. The Society for the Protection of Ancient Buildings and the Art Workers Guild, which he helped found continue to thrive. Even in the sphere of literature, where his reputation has perhaps suffered the steepest decline, C.S. Lewis and Tolkien claimed his late prose romances like 'The Wood Beyond The World' as an important inspiration for their own epic fictions. So, why has his public reputation failed to move much beyond his wallpaper?

¶G.K. Chesterton once remarked, considering why Morris's poems were no longer read: "If his poems were too like wallpapers, it was because he really could make wallpapers." Morris's design work, once so revolutionary, has over the years become practically a by-word for English bourgeois good taste. It is everywhere and rarely in contexts which Morris could have forseen, still less approved. In her magnificent fig-pudding of a biography, Fiona McCarthy[1] believes a whole cultural history could be written in terms of Morris furnishings and makes a good case by listing all those people whose homes were Morris & Co shrines: Oscar Wilde, George Bernard Shaw, the Webbs, the Pankhursts, Aldous Huxley, T.E. Lawrence, J.M. Keynes, John Betjeman, Kenneth Clark. This has meant that for a lot of people there seems to be a troublesome contradiction between Morris the social visionary and Morris the savvy businessman, supplying expensive goods to the houses of the rich and famous.

[1] p 413 William Morris, Fiona McCarthy (Faber & Faber, 1994)

⁋There are two things to be said here. The first is that Morris himself was painfully aware of the contradiction. Here he is responding to the charge in a public meeting in 1886 that he should give a his money away to the poor:

> I started in business for myself over thirty years ago. I am as rich now as I was when I began, despite my ability and industry. I have paid my men good wages — better, indeed, than they could get anywhere else. I have taught them to make beautiful things and some of the work which has passed through our hands will last even after our bones have mingled with the dust. I have treated my workmen not as an employer but as a comrade.
>
> ⁋I am not a rich man, but even if I were to give all my money away, what good would that do? The poor would still be just as poor, the rich, perhaps, a little more rich, for my wealth would finally get into their hands. The world would be pleased to talk to me for three days until something new caught its fancy. Even if Rothschild gave away his millions tomorrow, the same problems would confront us the day after.

⁋Spot on (and the rest of the crowd thought so, too). It's a splendid and thoughtful riposte to the tired old charge of hypocrisy by someone who has actually had a vision and made it happen in the real world.

⁋The second point to be made is that Morris was quite unlike the other public figures of his day. The appeal of his writing and speeches is that they bear the authentic thumbprint of the practitioner. He was driven mad by the use to which some of his work was put: "Do you suppose I like that kind of house! I would like a house like a big barn, where one ate in one corner, cooked in another corner, slept in a third corner and in the fourth, received one's friends." His own houses were, literally, works of art, because the revolutionary core of Morris's thought, the bit that still ought to speak to us, is that art begins at home, in the making and furnishing of a house. True art for Morris, is indistinguishable from craft: it isn't abstract "self-expression" but collective labour that gives pleasure in the doing and creates the beauty within which everyone had an equal right to live. Art for life's sake. Listen to this, from his pamphlet 'The Aims of Art':

> Art will utterly perish, as in the manual arts so in literature, which will become, as it is indeed speedily becoming, a mere string of orderly and calculated ineptitudes and passionless ingenuities; Science will grow more and more one-sided, more incomplete, more wordy and useless, till at last she will pile herself up into such a mass of superstition, that beside it the theologies of old time will seem mere reason and enlightenment. All will get lower and lower, till the heroic struggles of the past to realize hope from year to year, from century to century, will be utterly forgotten, and man will be an indescribable being – hopeless, desireless, lifeless.

¶Sound familiar? Literary novels that no one reads. A culture where no one knows how to make anything. Scads of scientific papers that only one or two specialists can understand. Lowest common denominator television. Social networking sites where people make "friends" they never meet. A society that doesn't remember the past and numbs itself with drink and drugs in order to face the future.

ORRIS often gets taken to task for being naïve, but he saw what was on its way far more clearly than any of his contemporaries (even as a teenager he refused to go into the Great Exhibition of 1851 with rest of his family, suspecting, quite rightly, that it would be brimful of industrial ugliness and wasteful luxury goods). In 1869, long before the Labour Party had been founded, he foresaw the split that would one day bring us New Labour:

> [I wonder] whether, in short, the tremendous organization of civilized commercial society is not playing the cat and mouse game with us socialists. Whether the Society of Inequality might not accept quasi-socialist machinery ... and work it for the purpose of upholding that society in a somewhat shorn condition, maybe, but a safe one ... the workers better treated, better organised, helping to govern themselves, but with no more pretence to equality with the rich, nor nay more hope for it than they have now.

❡The cynics – and they've had the upper hand for more than a century now – would say he was just another naïve Utopian, whose medieval-tinged sentimentality has been overtaken by the harsh lessons of history. Tosh.

⟨ Morris was tough, a player. He saw things for what they were but refused to be cowed by difficulty, or the mean-spiritedness of others. He just happened to have worked out that real satisfaction and pleasure derived from doing and making, not pontificating or amassing wealth. He was the first major cultural figure to say that art was for everyone or it was worthless. He left the world a much richer place than he entered it, physically and spiritually; he was funny; he was generous; he was kind. He was endlessly attentive to his children and he dealt with his wife's two long affairs with a tact and a generosity that still astonishes us today, in our so-called sexually liberated society. He didn't coin the phrase "the personal is political", but he damn well lived it.

⟨ Tell me if this doesn't cheer you up as vision for the working day:

> But, look suppose people could be in the country in five minutes walk, and had few wants; almost no furniture for instance and no servants, and studied (the difficult) arts of enjoying life, and finding out what they really wanted: then I think one might hope civilization had really begun.

Or this:

> I have never been in any rich man's house which would not have looked the better for having a bonfire made outside of it of nine-tenths of all that it held. Indeed, our sacrifice on the side of luxury will, it seems to me, be little or nothing: for, as far as I can make out, what people usually mean by it,

98

BUT, look suppose people could be in the country in five minutes walk, and had few wants; almost no furniture for instance and no servants, and studied (the difficult) arts of enjoying life, and finding out what they really wanted: then I think one might hope civilization had really begun. ❀❀❀❀❀ William Morris

is either a gathering of possessions which are sheer vexations to the owner, or a chain of pompous circumstance, which checks and annoys the rich man at every step. Yes, luxury cannot exist without slavery of some kind or other, and its abolition will be blessed, like the abolition of other slaveries, by the freeing both of the slaves and of their masters.

So direct, so wise and so true.

¶Reading Morris, or looking at, touching or sitting on his work in all its myriad forms, inspires us, not because he has all the answers, but because he asks the right questions. He was a man who didn't bury his talents; he exploited them, used himself all up, and we are still reaping the benefits:

> I entreat you (however trite the words may be) to think that life is not empty nor made for nothing, and that the parts of it fit into one another in some way; and that the world goes on, beautiful and strange and dreadful and worshipful.

His final words were: "I want to get mumbo jumbo out of the world". We're with you, Topsy: we still do.

The digital typefaces used in the presentation of this essay are P22 Morris; Golden, Troy and Morris Ornaments. Designed by Richard Kegler, based on Morris's type designs for his Kelmscott Press books. P22 Type Foundry, Buffalo, NY www.p22.com

TOPSY TURVY

William Morris Gallery Under Threat

※◆※

HE William Morris gallery in Walthamstow is situated at the artist's family home from 1848 to 1856.
It is the only public museum devoted to Morris's
work and houses a collection of fabrics, wallpapers,
painted tiles, books from the Kelmscott Press, as
well as furniture by Morris's followers in the Arts and Crafts
Movement. The gallery was opened by Clement Atlee, and most of
the work was bequeathed on trust that it would be available to local
people. ⁋ Lately council cuts to the tune of £56,000 a year have led
to reduced opening hours and the redundancy in December 2007 of
the long-serving curator and keeper, Peter Cormack. As a result,
the local people in Waltham Forest have started a campaign to keep
the museum open. ⁋ Katherine Green of the campaign says that
she has detected an ideological flavour to the council's atttitude:
"The council are very keen that the museum being used as a
wedding venue to generate funds. Whilst we are all acutely aware of
the difficulty in financing such organisations, the council has been
offered financial support from many sources to help keep the
gallery open for a year while it's reviewed, they've turned down
many offers of help from people with experience in arts and
cultural industry. They've been offered and turned down so much
help, that it's becoming bizarre. ⁋ "The previous council chief exec
referred to William Morris as a 'white imperialist', the current
council leader said in a speech that Morris is 'just an old dead white
man' – though he's since denied this. It's leading to many local
people thinking this is also an issue between old socialism and New
Labour."

✠

Go to www.keepourmuseumsopen.org.uk for the latest news on the campaign.

QI: DOWN WITH SCHOOL

John Mitchinson proposes a new
system of education

L ET'S START AT THE BEGINNING. WHAT IS SCHOOL FOR, DO
you think? Having taken on board that "education, education, education" is
the most important of all social priorities, why, actually, do we send our
children to school? I think the Rt Hon Gordon Brown would say (without a hint of
irony or shame) that it's to ensure we have a skilled workforce that keeps the UK
competitive in an increasingly global economy. Middle-class parents are likely to
witter on about "stretching" and "challenging" Sophie or Tobes, which really means
buying them the right (i.e. high achieving) peer group by taking them out of the
state system altogether. Everyone else will say they send their kids to school in the
vain hope they'll get a better paid job than their own, and in the meantime, it
keeps them off the streets.

If this sounds depressing, it's meant to. There isn't much to get excited about in
the current education debate — certainly nothing about, in William Morris's
words, setting "the true ideal of a full and reasonable life" before our children.
Education has degenerated, for all the well-meaning platitudes, into a purely
economic process, a production line for the consumer society. Nor is it just us
polite social revolutionaries saying this. Here's Professor Stephen Ball of London
University's Institute of Education, in his recently published book, *The Education
Debate:*

> Education is a servant to the economy. Education is now thoroughly subor-
> dinated to the supposed inevitabilities of globalisation and international
> economic competition.

And Sally Tomlinson, senior research fellow at the department of educational
studies at Oxford University:

> Education has moved from being a pillar of a welfare state, as intended by
> the postwar Labour government, to being a prop for a ruthless global
> market economy, which richly rewards winners and is draconian in its
> treatment of losers.

Both come to the same staggering conclusion: that for all the endless "radical initiatives" (459 documents on literacy strategy alone in the past seven years) and the billions of pounds of investment, the educational system today is as segregated in class terms as it was in William Morris's day. The middle classes have been the main beneficiaries from post-war educational policy, much as they have gained most from the National Health Service, but even they don't believe that state education has "improved". In fact, it's one of the great paradoxes of modern life that despite education being every right-thinking parent's "number one priority" and the "key to our nation's future", if you mention it in polite company, people's eyes immediately glaze over. As a conversational gambit, it's right up there with "health and safety" or house prices. If it is discussed at all, it's only ever in the context of fear: fear that standards are slipping, and that our children know less than we do; fear that you've made the wrong choice of school or fear that what they learn has no relevance to modern life and our children are becoming "unteachable".

Most of us resort to a strange form of sympathetic magic when it comes to schooling our young. Because we went through it and survived, then it follows our children should, too. But the "didn't do me any harm" school, as well as being dishonest and foolish, is also wasteful. What do we brave survivors have to show for those 2,535 classroom days (that's about 40% of our whole life up to the age of 17)? What do you remember from school? Most of us would probably recall one or two good teachers, some successes and many humiliations, the ebb and flow of friendships, the torture of exams. But what about the actual lessons? Try it: sit down and make a list of the first ten things that loom out of the murk. Then examine your list and see whether it passes muster as either useful or interesting. Unless you are gifted with a photographic memory you'll be staring at a rag-bag of half-grasped theories, fragments of other peoples' books and a soupy residue of "facts", many of them not even true. It's no wonder that so many of the great innovators; from Einstein and Edison to Bertrand Russell and Churchill, never, in the words of the latter, "let school interfere with their education". School favours conformists with retentive memories — Tony Blair was a star pupil at Fettes College; William Morris was considered unteachable by Marlborough.

It makes you wonder if school is of any use at all? In 1971 Austrian philosopher Ivan Illich published *Deschooling Society,* a slim bombshell of a book which remain as trenchant and relevant as ever:

> We cannot go beyond the consumer society unless we first understand that obligatory public schools inevitably reproduce such a society, no matter what is taught in them.

Illich made the simple but unavoidable point that if we really want to develop the potential of the greatest number of our fellow citizens, large, institutionalised schools are a disaster. You can change the curriculum as many times as you like, but all you are going to turn out, in the end, is consumers, people with limited inner resources and few skills who are united by the sole fact that they continually want more than they need. The "education debate" has skewered itself on this stark truth ever since: school doesn't change society; it reflects it. Illich's radical solution was to get rid of compulsory schooling altogether. Instead of homogenizing educational "funnels", Illich said we needed to reverse the process and create "educational *webs* which heighten the opportunity for each one to transform each moment of his living into one of learning." Easier said than done, of course, but the idea of a web of peers with similar interests and learning that continues throughout the whole of one's life are now mainstream ideas. What's more digital technology and the Web have made them a reality, accessible in every home and classroom.

Which is where QI comes in. We are, if nothing else, a web of peers. The books, TV shows, web pages we produce are really just the waste product of a group of non-specialists in remote locations attempting to educate themselves about the way the universe works. To find the good stuff, the stuff you remember because it's interesting or funny, involves behaving a bit like a disruptive pupil, the kind that is forever asking "Why?" It probably explains the TV show's popularity with school kids. It also explains the motivation for us to be so mad or presumptious to propose a QI school. Education, in one way or another, is what QI is all about. So, with the old joke about "If it's there you want, I wouldn't start from here" ringing in our ears, here's our plan. Imagine the status quo has melted away and we have a building, 100 bored children and no rules.

❖

The QI Prospectus

(i) *Play not work*

Have you noticed how even the kids who profess to hate school really like school trips and residential courses? It's that irresistible mixture of freedom and fun. Similarly, the kids that find lessons boring can find things online, build their own network of friends, make an interactive web page, build a playlist and write a blog without a second thought. Schools should be resource centres, not prisons. Teachers should be returned to their original roles as facilitators not bureaucrats or drill-masters. The more "work" resembles play — telling stories, making things — the more interested kids will become. This is hardly a new idea. 2,500 years ago, Plato wrote: "Let early education be a sort of amusement. You will then be better able to discover the natural bent."

Interestingly, the deep root of the word "teach" is "sign or mark". Teachers could be detectives, looking for the clues that makes each child tick. And "school" comes from the Greek, *skhole,* meaning "leisure or spare time".

(ii) *Follow the chain of curiosity*

Ask a kid about what they want to learn and they are unlikely to say "a broad-based curriculum that offers the core skills". Real learning is obsessive. It happens through watching, listening and practicing something that really interests you. That's Plato's "natural bent". What really captures your imagination? Maybe it's motorbikes. Maybe it's rabbits. Maybe it's Roald Dahl stories. Encourage children the freedom to follow their own curiosity right to the end of the chain and they will acquire the skills they need to get there. But wouldn't that lead to a classroom full of kids each doing their own thing? Yes. Wouldn't that be great?

People who derive deep satisfaction from their lives usually say things like: "From the age of five I knew I wanted to be a dancer," not "It was during literacy hour that I first realised reading was important". Jung was spot on here: "Children are educated by what the grown-up is and not by his talk".

(iii) *You decide*

The QI School isn't compulsory (it's either interesting or it isn't), and there are no exams, only projects or goals you set yourself with the teacher acting as a mentor. This could be making a film, or building a chair or cultivating a patch of ground. From age seven onwards, there would six navigation points which children would work around. Working on the "natural bent" theory, the time spent on each would differ from pupil to pupil, and from year to year.

- ❖ Philosophy — all seven year olds are instinctive cosmologists yet none of this speculation is covered or even much encouraged at school. By getting children to ask the big questions, to think about their thinking, this could encompass morality, current affairs, religion, politics, history and psychology, with the teachers adding context to the children's insights, either privately or in small groups. A QI School would have no use for intimidating assemblies.

- ❖ Storytelling — by drafting in professional oral storytellers, children would gain the skill and confidence to tell their own stories. Memory skills would be taught, so that poems, stories, songs and plays could be learnt and recited. Different — or so-called "dead" — cultures and languages would become interesting rather than odd, pointless or threatening. Family, ethnic and local histories would be integrated into the school organically, not through dread "outreach initiatives". And, finally, the real point of learning to read and write would be magically revealed.

- ❖ Music — singing, instruments, participation for all, opportunities for talented musicians to spend more time developing their skill.

- ❖ Technology — making, designing, understanding scientific methods, machines and the beauty of numbers.

- ❖ Nature — all the earth and life sciences — geology, geography, animals, plants, ecology, agriculture and environment.

- ❖ Games — plenty, from the usual ball sports through to more holistic practices like pilates, to ensure the broadest participation. Competition would be encouraged, but without the humiliation that so often accompanies it. And no "healthy eating initiatives", but QI investigations in to how the body works and why.

The idea is simple. Not all children are equally gifted at everything. Not all learn at the same speed; not all are interested in the same things. But all of them without exception are interested in something. So it's less about "teaching" them things you already know, but giving them the tools and confidence to find things out for themselves. As Joseph Campbell, the mythologist, put it: "The job of an educator is to teach students to see vitality in themselves."

(iv) *No theory without practice*

Each of these areas would be divided between reading, writing and talking on the one hand and doing and making on the other. If you're lost in your curiosity chain looking at, say, lettuce, as well as marvelling at its soporific qualities, or the fact you can extract rubber from it, or its sacred status among the Kurdish Yezidi tribe, you will want to have a go at growing it, too. The school would pull in local people who still have teachable skills (whether it's prize-winning vegetables, car maintenance, welding, making furniture, or editing documentaries) to inspire and instruct. It would be good for them, and potentially life changing for the children.

And we mean it about no exams. What are they for, other than making half the world feel useless? To establish a national standard which nobody trusts anymore? To help employers assess whether someone is suitable for a job? It's just an excuse for not taking responsibility, making eye contact and communicating with a fellow human being. Wouldn't it be better to ask a local candidate "why, really, do want to do this?" and then get them to show you what they've made, built, written, drawn or baked. Or, better still, to have spotted them at school already and taken them on, part-time. At the QI School local apprenticeships could be revived without costly government schemes and all their attendant blather and flannel.

(v) *You never leave*

Because most of us can't get out of school quickly enough, we have probably never thought about going back. What a waste! The QI School would be the centre of its community, dependent on parents and local people to make it work. And there is absolutely no reason why school has to stop dead at 17 (QI started when John Lloyd put himself back to school, aged 44, so he could help his children with their homework). The QI School is the ultimate "lifelong learning" venue, a mini-university (which, of course, once meant 'a place of wholeness'), where skills and knowledge could be pooled on- and off-line, and young and old could indulge their curiosity, and ask their difficult "why" questions, side by side, each learning from and challenging the other.

O F COURSE, this all sounds mad, impractical, and impossibly idealistic. Human beings are too lazy, mean and venal, surely? Maybe so, but is it any more mad than the wasteful, divisive mess most of us been legally compelled to endure for over a century? Schools, hospitals, army barracks and prisons may smell the same now, but they haven't always and don't need to in the future. The coming century is going to require all kinds of adjustments, most of them requiring a return to smaller, cheaper, smarter ways of living. The three-faced monster Education-education-education will have to change and it will be us, not the Government, who'll do the changing. If we need a rallying cry, we could do worse than W. B. Yeats prophetic words:

*Education is not the filling of a bucket,
but the lighting of a fire.*

Introducing a new system of measurement: common sense

'A full and convincing account of why our well-tried and trusted traditional measures make human sense'
Alexander McCall Smith

'Fun and fascinating – the secrets and tricks of how we measure the world around us'
Conn Iggulden

'Lucid and wise and touching and absolutely right'
Jilly Cooper

'His direct, engaging conversational prose is a delight to read . . . inspirational'
Andrew Roberts

ABOUT THE SIZE OF IT
The Common Sense Approach to Measuring Things

'Fun and fascinating – the secrets and tricks of how we measure the world around us'
Conn Iggulden

'A full and convincing account of why our well-tried and trusted traditional measures make human sense'
Alexander McCall Smith

WARWICK CAIRNS

THE TRUTH ISN'T
OUT THERE

History is an ever-changing collection of tales and fables,
says Justin Pollard, not a list of facts and dates

WHAT IS HISTORY? THAT'S WHAT I KEEP ASKING MYSELF. I don't mean in terms of an academic definition, I mean what is it made of and what do we think it's for? Ofsted recently found that two-thirds of children drop history aged 14, leading Katherine Tattersall of the Chartered Institute of Educational Assessors to say that "history is in decline". To me that's a bit like saying breathing is in decline, but I worry she might be right. Yet we have whole channels devoted to history programming which seem very popular, and American studios are still prepared to put big money into historical epics which they clearly believe have an audience and will make them money. So what's going on?

Personally I don't believe history can be in decline because it's a fundamental part of what we are, what we know, where we come from and, frankly, the only guide we have to what might happen in the future. We all use history every day, otherwise we wouldn't know who we are or where to go. Certainly some subjects can decline. I can imagine a time when David Beckham Studies loses its caché, but then David Beckham will simply become another subject for historians to look at. The fact that history in schools might be in decline I think implies a different problem and that has to do with what we think history is.

I believe that a history taught in terms in names, dates and "important events" can give us a skewed sense of what history is and this approach may be what is leading to the subject's reported decline. I don't think history should be simply a political commentary, I don't think memorizing names and dates is particularly useful and, most of all, I don't think history is about establishing a "correct" view of what happened because I don't think there is one.

As a historical writer and advisor for feature films I get to deal with "correct" views of history quite a lot. After any feature film or TV series I receive letters concerning this question, usually framed along the lines of:

Dear Idiot,

In [fill in name of movie here] you showed this character doing that. This character never did that. Everyone knows that. Except you, it would seem. You are an idiot.

Yours etc.

And to be honest they're right on just about every point except one — I did know. In fact I've rarely come across a major change to accepted historical narrative in a movie that the entire crew didn't know about. The reason we did something other than what my correspondent believed to be "correct" is that we had to get the gist of a story which might unfold over many years at a distant time and in a distant place into around two hours of on screen entertainment whilst maintaining a narrative that made sense to a modern audience and made the point that the film makers wanted to make. This involves editing the facts, or as some historians would have it — lying.

The big question of course is, in doing this, are we really lying? Are we misleading the public and giving them a false sense of historical events? Personally I don't think so. In the first place, whilst some of them may think I'm an idiot, I don't think most movie-goers are naïve enough to believe that they're watching a "home movie from the past" with events unfolding in real time just as they did in real life. They know they're in a theatre — the popcorn is a dead giveaway. Just as importantly, I don't think the past can actually be recreated in the way that some historical movie detractors would wish.

L.P. Hartley famously opened *The Go-Between* with the line "The past is a foreign country; they do things differently there", and he was absolutely right. The past is, at its deepest level, unknowable and unvisitable. We do not have a complete set of data on which to base it, nor can we just use our empathy to "imagine" what it was like to live there. It is impossible not to be the modern person you are with the modern knowledge you have and so you can never know what it was to be them. History, as such, is just a story created in the present about the past. What makes the difference between what any generation considers good history and bad history is simply the degree to which that story can be agreed upon.

History, as I like to think about it, is a mirror we hold up in the present and, as we walk into the future, we catch glimpses in it over our shoulder, of what lies in the past. It is not a true mirror, it bends and distorts depending on the ground we are treading on. As such each era has a different view and sees the past differently.

None is necessarily right, none is necessarily wrong and every history tells us as much about the present in which it was written as it does about the past it tries to describe. This is why every generation has the right to reinterpret history — to describe what they see in the mirror.

For anyone making historical movies, or writing historical books for that matter, there is a danger that some of our audience will say "wait a minute, that's wrong!". If they're talking about a detail that we can know about then they've got a point, but often they complain most about their own interpretations which they wish us to believe are not interpretations but "how it was".

To explore this point I've been spending some time giving myself false memories. Not big false memories you understand — nothing involving being Napoleon in a former life or believing I was once attacked by a dragon, just little ones. I got the idea for this from an article in *New Scientist* (issue 2622, 19 September 2007, page 34–41) on some research that Elizabeth Loftus has been doing at the University of California. Her work for the last thirty years has involved studying how the human mind can "create" memories to fill in the gaps in narratives it knows in an attempt to make sense of the world around it. We can have a go at it now if you like, using the Deese-Roediger-McDermott paradigm. First off read these two word lists:

LIST 1

apple, vegetable, orange, kiwi, citrus, ripe, pear, banana, berry, cherry, basket, juice, salad, bowl, cocktail

LIST 2

web, insect, bug, fright, fly, arachnid, crawl, tarantula, poison, bite, creepy, animal, ugly, feelers, small

Now cover up these lists and wait a few minutes — perhaps go and make a cup a tea. When you get back look at the third list below (no peeking at the other ones) and tick off all the words you remember from the first two:

LIST 3

happy, woman, winter, circus, spider, feather, citrus, ugly, robber, piano, goat, ground, cherry, bitter, insect, fruit, suburb, kiwi, quick, mouse, pile, fish.

Did you notice anything odd? Did you "remember" any words being on the first two lists that weren't actually there? "Spider" perhaps? Or "fruit"? It doesn't work for everyone but it did for me. I had a false memory. My mind, in trying to remember the lists it had seen before, did more than just recall, it recreated and in the process added a word which I could then have sworn was on the first lists.

But what does this have to do with making movies, other than sounding like a wheedling excuse for getting things wrong? My point in filling my head with imaginary spiders and fruit is that all history is a story in which a bare set of "facts" are woven into a narrative with the addition of material that comes not from then but from now and as such we can never know exactly what happened or how things were. We can try to be as accurate as we can but, fundamentally, there is no such thing as truth.

But this is not to say that there's no point to history — far from it. The academic study of history involves finding and interrogating sources of information and comparing those narratives that we and those before us have garnered from it to see if we can come up with a story that we all agree on. It's rather like a policeman taking witness statements after an accident. Every witness will have a different "memory" of exactly what happened although this does not mean that some are consciously lying. The job of the police is to discover if there is a version of these memories that can be agreed upon and hence provide the most likely explanation of events.

What worries me about some of the letters I get are not the corrections to detail, which are always welcome as we certainly do make mistakes from time to time, but the belief that there is a "true" version of events behind the story that is recoverable in its entirety and which we have got wrong — as opposed to there being many narratives and many ways of getting over the message that a writer wishes to make about a story from the past. It is this oppressive idea which states that history is just a dull block of facts that must be correctly learned and this which I think might put kids off history. It would certainly put me off.

To give another example not everyone agreed that I should have used one story in my last book, *The Interesting Bits – The History You Might Have Missed* as it "wasn't history". Here it is so you can make up your own mind:

The story goes that Collen was walking along one day, daydreaming about that time he'd killed a giantess, when a talking peacock came up to him, which was quite a surprise. The peacock then asked Collen if he'd care to have dinner with the King of the Fairies but three times the saint refused. The peacock was very persistent however, in the way that peacocks are, and eventually he agreed.

Collen duly rolled up at the king's place in his Sunday best and was initially rather impressed. The King of the Fairies seemed to live in a huge castle, with lots of servants and Collen was shown into a room where the King, like the ghost of Christmas Past, sat surrounded by an enormous quantity of food. However Collen wisely surmised that this was all a bit fishy so he reminded the King about the fate of the Godless and then started sprinkling Holy Water around like it was going out of fashion. Instantly the castle, the food and the King evaporated and all that was left was a demonic bird which then flew away forever.

Another version of the story has it that Collen was living in a cave near Glastonbury when he was asked to mediate in the age-old May-Day dispute between Gwynn ap Nudd, Lord of the Underworld, and Gwyther, Lord of Summer, for the hand of the fair Creiddylad, the Maiden of Spring. The Lord of the Underworld was very insistent but the friends of the lord of Summer pointed out quite rightly that the year above ground would drag somewhat if spring went off with him. At this point St. Collen arrived and told them both that he would settle their dispute but they'd have to wait until the day he chose. They agreed and then he chose Doomsday which was a neat trick. There followed a liberal dousing with Holy Water and, as before, all the pixies and fairies of the ancient Gods disappeared.

Now this hagiographic tale seems to make some fairly spectacular departures from what we might call history. Talking peacocks seems rather unlikely, there is sadly precious little proof of the existence of fairies or pixies and castles rarely disappear without the aid of gunpowder. This much we can probably agree on. Some might dispute other elements as well—are there really such things as saints?—can you do magic with Holy Water?—can birds be "demonic"? We might also doubt that there ever was a St. Collen as the main proof of his existence comes from this fabulous hagiography.

Considering all this there are many who would argue that such a story has no place in a history book. But I think it does. I'm interested in why the writer of the hagiography would choose these stories and I think the choice tells us something about what he thought his audience needed or wanted to know. It's intriguing that there was clearly a need at the time to explain why the seasons happened, which in the absence of firm astronomical data, this story did. For the readers or listeners to this story at the time of its writing, this was history — it made sense, it explained things and it provided a narrative within which it could all be remembered. That *is* history and in discussing it we learn as much about the world of the writer of the story and the world of today as we do about the slightly odd world of St. Collen himself, if it ever existed. It's true that I'd worry about anyone reciting this tale to me as "fact", but the problem would lie not in the story but in their uncritical analysis of it.

The same goes for movies. Directors and writers usually take up old stories because they have something to say about them or believe the stories have something to say about us and not because they want to re-enact the past. Making a ten-year long movie in which everything about Ivan the Terrible's life was lovingly recreated in as much detail as possible is not the same thing as telling the story of Ivan the Terrible and it's not, I believe, what the film-makers or the audience would want. It is a story in which many things will be changed and I don't believe that is a problem. I am more suspicious of a documentary re-enactment which claims to be "true" than a movie in which Elizabeth I rides a skateboard.

I am all in favour of those movie-goers who, at the end of two hours shout "I don't believe you!" and I hope very much that some of the audience might want to learn more about the period and characters when they leave the theatre but I do object to those who would censor popular history based on what they "know" happened. That way lies all the sterility and boredom of the school of history teaching that says it's all about names and dates, about facts and figures, about truth. History is about understanding stories, about narrative, and there is a place in it for the full spectrum of experience and interpretation as it is only through reading the more fabulous tales that we can come to an understanding of our sources and what they are trying to tell us. This, in my opinion, is what history is about — about developing the tools to interrogate the stories from the world around us, be they in history books, movies, newspaper articles or rolling news items. And to enjoy the stories, particularly the wild ones, for I think they tell us most about ourselves and make our history enjoyable and engaging. We should never simply believe them, but equally we should never give in to those who would tell us that they "know" how it was — because they don't.

❖

Ten of History's Wildest Stories

1 Miss Canary Islands 1936 being … General Franco.

2 Hannah Twynnoy being eaten by a tiger in 1703 — in a pub — in Malmesbury.

3 Mrs Walter Raleigh introducing her friends to her husband after he's been executed (she carried his head around in a bag).

4 Sir Alured's wife disappearing in a puff of perfume, leaving only her clothes behind.

5 George Washington being asked to become King of America.

6 The weevils of St. Julien winning their own estate to live on in a court case in 1587.

7 The last UK prosecution under the 1735 Witchcraft Act being in 1944.

8 The late Pope Formosus being dug up, dressed in his papal robes and tried for heresy.

9 William the Conqueror exploding in his coffin.

10 Hilter drawing the poster for 'Teddy's Perspiration Powder'.

Find out more in Mr Pollard's *The Interesting Bits: The History You Might Have Missed* (John Murray, 2006)

✧

MY OWN GREEN HILLS

Elizabeth Garner contemplates the number seven,
and finds freedom from enclosure

"Give me a child until he is seven,
and I will give you the man."

S O GOES THE WELL-KNOWN JESUIT SAYING, IMPOSSIBLE NOW TO separate from the acclaimed *Seven Up!* series, which charted the fortunes of seven children from diverse backgrounds. Part social study, part soap opera, we saw a range of personalities emerging against the radical cultural and political changes of 1964 to 2002. We saw dreams realised, ambitions quashed. And yet, really, were those lives already predetermined by those personality traits shown in that first episode?

My experience in the TV and film industry over the past ten years makes me doubt this version of reality. How can we see the essential nature of any individual if he or she is performing for the camera? How can a story be entirely true if a life is edited into soundbites to create entertainment? Now our "real life" human soap operas are synonymous with manipulation and humiliation: the world of *Big Brother* which, also, began as a social experiment but has degenerated into a claustrophobic freak show where participants equate popularity with sexual titillation. The payoff for the audience: the sense that no matter how hard our lives may be, at least we are not as selfish, dysfunctional or aggressive as these specimens of humanity. And the Faustian reward for the participants: the opportunity to be someone. But this "someone" is a further illusion: it's a persona created by the viewers, a set of pre-selected traits that are expected from our reality fodder. It is not the essence of the individual being celebrated—which should, surely, be the true nature of celebrity.

This need for stories to be created from the lives of others is not a modern phenomenon. The trend for "social pages" of the newspaper really gathered force in the 19th century: as the wealthy middle-classes created complex codes of behaviour, the poorer public delighted in the morally satisfying tales of self-made fortunes and good marriages. As the Industrial Revolution lead to shifts in the boundaries of class and culture, the public fixated on these reported "real lives" as an example of how to navigate the new social landscape. But now our moral tales lack any satisfactory conclusion. We watch the horrors of happy-slapping available on Youtube. Parents are blamed in abstract; and the government seeks to employ legislative measures of asbos. As if dictating to a teenager how they ought to be is the solution to correcting undesirable behaviour. Meanwhile, if the Jesuits are to be believed, then in twenty years time the world will be run by uneducated, intractable, alcoholic adults, prone to outbreaks of mass violence, broadcasting their brutality for the world to see. Some might say we have already reached this point of no return.

This seven year theory also emerges in Oliver James' book *They Fuck You Up*. He asserts that a child's personality is formed in the first seven years of his life — not through innate genetic make-up, but through a combination of determining factors: parents, peers, and external stimulus. Children by nature run wild: what they run wild into is a complex environment over which we, as adults, must surely have some control. But, if the seven year theory is to be believed, then aren't we just as doomed, repeating patterns of behaviour that were established before we learnt how to read, think and act for ourselves? Are we not, then on some terrible production-line of dysfunction?

This argument is a disturbingly convincing edit of our modern world: selecting a story and shaping the facts the fit it, in order to provide maximum shock value. It also encourages a certain level of passivity: this is the way we are. Whether it's the fate of our children or the fate of the planet, it's inevitable, we might as well just sit back and watch the apocalypse on our plasma TV screens. At least it'll be a bit more comfortable here, with the door locked.

But what if this desire to shut ourselves away from the evils of the world is also part of the problem? In a recent visit to the Barbican I saw storyteller Hugh Lupton perform *Common Ground*, a remarkable retelling of the life of John Clare, the peasant poet who came of age during the time of the Enclosure Acts. Clare wrote with sensual accuracy about the lithe, ever-changing nature of the country-side. He became renowned at the very time that the land he loved was enclosed by men who "Turned my own green hills about / And pickt my very bones." Clare was eventually committed to the madhouse due to conditions brought about by a tendency to "poetical prosing." So far, so tragic: another tale of the artist being consumed by his own genius. Dylan Thomas did it; Francis Bacon did it — the inevitability of the personality type.

However, Lupton provides a broader context for this story of the poet's decline. He begins with an explanation of how the combination of family and fable lead him to tell the tale of John Clare. He cites the Native American proverb: that the full implications of our actions will only be understood in seven generations' time. He then describes how he drew a family tree for his daughters, tracing his seventh generation back to Clare's time: 1793–1864. As he tells the tale of Clare's descent into madness he does not present it as a self-perpetuated internal condition. The mind is not an isolated entity, it is profoundly affected by the immediate environment. Clare lost his sense of place, and therefore lost his sense of self. Projecting the logic of the Enclosures seven generations ahead Lupton illuminates the nature of our present common land: the concrete jungles of the shopping malls where adults consume and children congregate. We, like Clare, have become divorced from our own natural landscape and are enclosed by economic forces. As such, we are also slowly losing our minds.

This seems a bold assertion until we begin to follow that chain of cause and effect across the years. Before the Enclosures act, the rural communities thrived through a sense of connection. The Lord of the estate gained his wealth from his tenants, but that wealth was directly related to a sense of place, and to the whims of the seasons. The rich and poor lived within the same boundaries of the land, and both were involved in the rites and rituals of the passing year. This shared awareness gave the landowner a sense of place in larger cosmic order, and a sense of very practical responsibility: if the workers were not cared for, the land would suffer, if the land suffered then the Harvest would fail and the profit would be less. The access to common land allowed the workers some sense of freedom and self-sufficiency. Their animals could graze , and they could harvest. They had a very practical, immediate connection to their place: they cared for the land and the land cared for them.

Once the land was enclosed, the workers could not survive. The only viable option was to seek work at the mills and factories of the nearby towns, where new industries abounded. The brutal tales of mechanised workforce of the industrial revolution are well documented. Within one generation, families were uprooted from the place of their ancestors and confined in inhumane conditions, shut away from the rhythms of the seasons, solely dependent on the factory to provide their income.

At the same time, the city became a place of opportunity for the middle-classes. Invention and mass-production lead to self-made wealth: a good idea could make a man rich in a matter of months. Status became defined by what you had achieved in the present, and your vision for the future, rather than just being able to trace an ancient family lineage back to the past. This new money created a huge market for the trinkets and fashions that are the symbols of disposable income. A place in the countryside became a further demonstration of success, added to the very practical fact that it was much more pleasant for the factory owners to be as far away as possible from the stench and smoke of the industry. The Master physically separated himself from his workers, and rarely saw the human price he paid to gain his fortune.

In this manner, in the space of twenty years , the blueprint for our modern society was drawn up. The events that mark out the following century can all be seen as inevitable progressions of this shift in the social model: War; economic depression; Thatcherite government; Climate Change. Suddenly Lupton's claim seems all too plausible. We live in crowded cities, shielded from our environment by the technologies of modern entertainment. We laugh at, and judge, the community that arrives in our living room through the voyeuristic power of television, but do not connect with the people who live side by side with us. We work long hours to obtain the money, or the credit rating, needed to have the latest gadget, the latest fashion, the ultimate holiday. At the same time, we are beset by allergies and neuroses and we worry about the drinking, violence and promiscuity that the papers tell us are rife in the next generation.

So what is to be done? Is the only answer a retreat back to nature, forming communities around a patch of land? In part, yes. Last year it was reported the highest amount of seeds bought for self-production since World War II: allotment-culture is booming. It seems our disposable income is not simply being snatched from us by the power of advertising. We are creatures of habit, but we are also innately self-correcting. If there is an imbalance in our environment, there is something in us that wants to change it for the better. In my own experience, I am involved in a community garden project, which, amongst other things, provides the opportunity for individuals with depression to grow their own produce. There is no doubt that the experience of tending vegetables through the seasons provides an opportunity to break the internal cycles of mental distress: it allows a tangible, practical reconnection with a world outside oneself. The gathering of disparate people working towards a common aim, rather than enclosed and defined by a common illness, is also a vital ingredient to this process of rehabilitation.

But grass-roots life is not the solution for everyone. And in this context, the technology that is all too easy to dismiss as a curse can also be seen as a blessing: a patch of land can take on many forms. It can be a virtual community on the internet. It can be a magazine subscribed to by a handful of enthusiasts. It can be a manifesto discussed at the pub with a bunch of friends. The point is, whatever we care about can and should connect us with others. And this is what should define us, rather than aspiring to the mirage of celebrity status: of becoming "someone" defined by the ever-critical gaze of the media. But in a world where the mechanisms of society and industry tell us how to spend our time and money, it is vital that we actively seek out that connection for ourselves, rather than passively consume whatever we are told is desirable.

If we are creatures that are formed by our environment — socially, psychologically and geographically — then it is important to remember that we can also challenge and change that environment every day. Seven years is not a life sentence. In fact, it is a time frame that repeats in intriguing patterns throughout our culture. Shakespeare gave us Seven Ages of Man; astrology makes much of the seven-year pattern of Saturn Returns and, intriguingly, scientific studies have shown that the human skin sheds and regenerates on a seven year cycle. We are not the same people in 2008 that we were in 2001. And, as such, we can choose what we build and what we destroy, and what patterns we set in motion for the next seven generations. It is simply a matter of unlocking our doors and seeking out the common ground.

Hugh Lupton: www.angelfire.com/folk/hughlupton

A BIT OF MAGIC

David Boyle is away with the fairies

Illustrated by Alice Smith

*"I haven't seen any fairy people," said a disappointed lady next to me.
"And I've brought my wings too!"*

WE ARE IN A CORNER OF BODMIN MOOR IN CORNWALL AND I have arrived rather too early for the first ever fairy festival in the UK. It is damp and vast men with William Morris tattoos are asking if I have registered for camping. But the stage is up and there are people dressed as fairies, and playing a range of sparkly new age instruments, practising on it. Organiser Karen Kay, a member of the "pagan vocal group" Daughters of Gaia, is at reception, a garland of flowers around her head, ticking people off a long list.

A man dressed somewhere between Gandalf and Paraceslus is creeping along the small queue towards us, leaning heavily on his staff.

The lady with the wings needn't have worried. Within a couple of hours, there are nearly 400 fairy enthusiasts, of all shapes, ages, classes and genders, many of them sporting a variety of different wings—some of them also with wands and tinsel.

I pass two rather delicate-looking ladies of a certain age, ordering drinks at the bar, whose wings were so diaphanous and whose angelic make-up so extensive, that they must have been preparing their appearance for days. I hope the rain holds off for them, but suspect it won't.

There are stalls selling everything from fortune-telling to fairy shoes—tiny, delicate and carved, the size of ear-rings. On stage for the next three days will be Kate Bush's cousin Beck Sian, 'fairy vocalist' Priscilla Hernandez from Spain, and the 'fairy harpist' Elizabeth Jane Baldry.

It is a peculiar experience for me. I normally exist firmly in the metropolitan world of think-tanks and politics, with the occasional foray into writing history books. Yet here I am, near Jamaica Inn, amidst a flurry of wands, wings, long striped socks, pointed shoes, garlands of flowers and what you might call Greenpeace chic.

What am I doing here, wingless and looking horribly like the serious London writer I pretend to be, amidst such frivolity? Partly because there is something enormously refreshing somehow, putting aside all the extremes of affectation, to be with 400 people dressed like fairies when I know, in Whitehall, we have the most utilitarian government since they stuffed Jeremy Bentham. Somehow, a few hours at the 3 Wishes Fairy Festival is, for me, the antidote to Tesco, BAA and the *Financial Times*.

But I also have an excuse. I am a trend watcher and there is no doubt that this is a trend. There is another Cornish fairy event set for the autumn, and this event is one of at least twelve major festivals worldwide dedicated to fairies this summer — from Queencreek, Arizona to Slippery Rock, Pennsylvania; from Guelph, Ontario to French Lick, Indiana. There are two big fairy exhibitions, in Canada and Philadelphia.

Something is in the air. Just when you thought it was safe at the bottom of the garden — when the whole notion of the "little people" had been consigned to effete affectation — the idea of fairies seems to be making a comeback. What is going on?

❖

IT IS HARD TO OVER-ESTIMATE JUST HOW UNFASHIONABLE FAIRIES HAVE become in the UK during the 20th century. They had a good start thanks to the combined Edwardian talents of Arthur Rackham and J. M. Barrie. *Peter Pan* was first shown to rapturous applause in 1904. In fact, there is some evidence that fairies tend to enjoy their revivals at the turns of centuries (*Midsummer Night's Dream* 1595/6, Coleridge's *Song of the Pixies* 1793). But something about the whole Tinkerbell thing—the delicate femininity, the questionable childish sexuality — did not mix well with the century to come.

When Arthur Conan Doyle published the Cottingly fairy photographs in 1921 — the very obvious fakes made by two little girls in Yorkshire — they had the very opposite effect on later generations that he intended. One look at the dancing gnome, or the obvious brassieres, was enough to turn fairies into a laughing stock. Though one of the girls maintained until she died that they had faked the photographs because nobody believed them when they *had* seen fairies.

Six years later, Sir Quentin Craufurd founded the Fairy Investigation Society, designed to promote serious study. Over the years, it managed to attract a number of prominent supporters, including Walt Disney and the Battle of Britain supremo Air Chief Marshal Lord Dowding, whose career was not helped by his public expressions of belief.

But by the 1970s, the Society could stand the cynical public climate no longer and it went underground. I wrote to their last known address outside Dublin some years ago, when I was first interested in these things, and had a strange letter back. It was from a man claiming that he knew the society's secretary, but he said he didn't want to talk to anybody. Not only the fairies had disappeared, but the fairy researchers seem to have fled as well.

No wonder fairies were unfashionable.

I know one folklorist who spent years trying to write a thesis on belief in the Banshee — a rather noisy aspect of the fairy legend — in contemporary Ireland, but couldn't find anyone who did believe in it (luckily, the university cleaner happened to mention that she had heard one the night before).

I wrote a novel for adults about fairies a few years ago, based on the same theory that there are fairy revivals when centuries turn. There was some interest from the big publishers in publishing it, but only on condition that I took out the fairies. Since that was really the whole point, I declined.

But despite all that, something has been going on out there to bring the hopelessly unfashionable back into fashion, subtly and below the radar of the chattering classes in London.

Just how far below the radar is sometimes uncomfortably apparent. My novel is now published (*Leaves the World to Darkness*) and it is selling, but not everybody immediately understands the point. "I was very interested by some of your articles on your website," said a successful businessman I met for the first time recently. "But," he said, looking at me as if some frilly knickers had popped out of my breast pocket, "fairies?"

Even so, the coming of the fairies is not happening entirely outside mainstream culture. The Royal Academy ran a highly successful exhibition of Victorian fairy paintings in 1998, which went on to acclaim at the Frick in New York, the University of Iowa and the Art Gallery of Ontario in Toronto. Susanna Clarke's brilliant novel *Jonathan Strange & Mr Norrell* also has a prominent role for a fairy. She herself points to *Buffy the Vampire Slayer* as a key influence.

The Daughters of Gaia's website even has a message of congratulatory enthusiasm from the distinguished professor of history at Bristol University, Ronald Hutton (who has, incidentally, described the fairy revival as the "British religion").

There are also whole orchestras of people describing themselves as "fairy musicians". There is a new magazine, published in Maryland, called *Fairie*, and enough new fairy websites to re-populate Google. There is even an American attempt to re-brand Midsummer's Day as "Fairy Day".

The key question is this. We live in a society so technocratic that the only solution to high cancer mortality rates anyone seems to be able to suggest is more robots — why, in those circumstances, are fairies staging such a comeback?

We have lived with the angels sub-culture for ten years or more, but that was directly spiritual and — if you really bought into it — well, you could get your deepest desires granted. But, as the businessman said — fairies? Fairies are a bit less practical, and a good deal less fashionable to start with

But there are some clues if we go back to the 3 Wishes Fairy Festival, and its very distinctive style — dungeons and dragons by way of Botticelli — and its array of small businesses offering music, books and spells.

These are not the dark fairies you might read about in Christina Rossetti's *Goblin Market*, or in Susanna Clarke's stories either. This is more like a glittery and diaphanous branch of the New Age. We are talking optimistic, light-bearing fairies, bringing the natural world to life

Festival organiser Karen Kay, a former broadcast journalist, says it's about concern for the environment. She's probably right. You might wonder whether dressing in wings — still less driving to Bodmin Moor — is going to get the job done. But then again, the business of re-injecting something mystic, and profoundly non-aggressive, into the world can't be such a bad thing. And there does seem to be something about fairies which not only recognises the mystery, hidden life and sheer magic of woods, forests and the natural world, but which also flies in the face of brute fact.

"A man can't always *do* as he likes," said John Ruskin in his Slade lecture "Fairyland" in 1893, "but he can always *fancy* what he likes."

One of the problems for 20th century audiences was, of course, that Ruskin did rather fancy fairies — or at least their human equivalent. But let's leave that on one side. The point is that fairies were for him, and maybe also for us, an antidote to grim reality.

Maybe the very depth of our official technocratic cynicism — where Richard Dawkins' scepticism can be a major bestseller — has its own equal and opposite reaction. In a dull concrete world, which seems determined to engulf what remains of those woods and forests, some of us do long for a bit of magic. In fact, that is the most human reaction to climate disaster.

I'm not sure fairies are quite the antidote we need to slay Dawkins-style fundamentalism. I'm not sure that any number of pairs of diaphanous fairy wings would melt the heart of the Treasury. But we do need magic in our lives — and the hope of a little mystery — and, for that reason, I'm backing the fairies.

Do I actually believe in them?

There is a fascinating story of a fairy encounter in Janet Bord's book *Fairies: Real Encounters with Little People* about a strange experience reported in 1973 near Alderwasley in the Amber Valley in Derbyshire.

Suddenly, next to a grassy bank on a beautiful summer's day, there was a four-foot green man. The witness describes a short conversation, during which the fairy — if indeed that's what he was — said that his work involved breaking down decaying material for food for plants. Other twentieth century witnesses have talked about fairies claiming that they are helping trees to grow.

I'm not saying these people were necessarily reliable witnesses for a crown court trial. Nor am I saying that I would go to the stake in defence of their sanity. But the idea appeals to me.

If fairies are some hidden aspect of natural processes, the personification of rotting or photo-synthesis in a parallel reality, then — yes, maybe I can believe in them. Whether these processes also have some power over human luck, as fairies are traditionally supposed to have, well — who knows.

Certainly I prefer to live in a world where there are parallel ways of looking at reality, just as there are shades of opinion, than the miserable cut-and-dried Blairite world I seem to have been born into.

Will this admission help my career in the world of think-tanks and politics? Almost certainly not. But, when all is said and done, we do need to stand up for a bit of magic.

*David Boyle is a fellow at the New Economics Foundation
and the author of a novel about fairies called*
Leaves the World to Darkness
(www.therealpress.co.uk)

Tommy, born free and is everywhere in CHAINS

by Bron Jones

and you, gathering in.
you were small
        You were BORN

and you flew between
the atoms as if you
knew the way

passing the shores
of our excellence

and the echo of our
expensive emptiness

fists holding the
LIGHT
and eyes that
KNEW the path
you came by

until they OPENED

AND
BEGAN
HUNGER

TOMMY TOMMY
LOOK , **LOOK**

what Mummy's
got.
TOMMY LOOK
LOOK LOOK

LOOK TOMMY ,
LOOK , TOMMY'S
truck........ ahhh
look at him LOOKING....
he's LOOKING at his TRUCK

TOMMY!
what have you
~~learnt~~ so far?
That your name
is TOMMY.
You ARE tommy,
and the TRUCK
is YOURS

Tommy
me
truck

Good boy

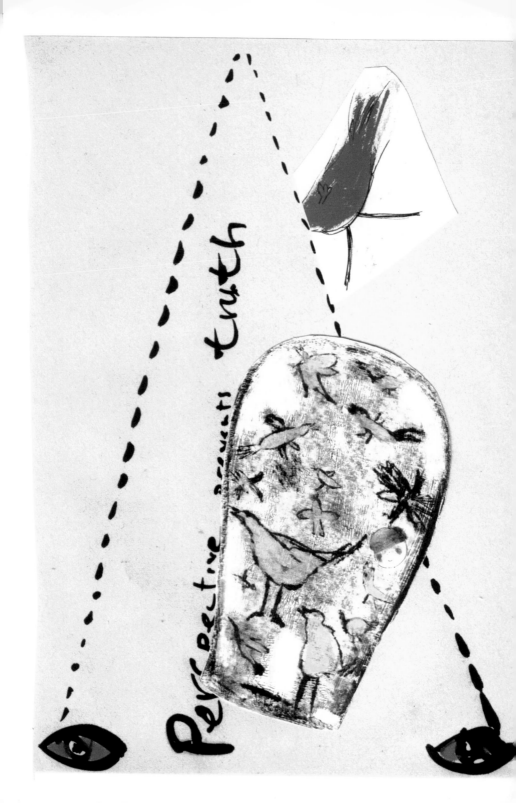

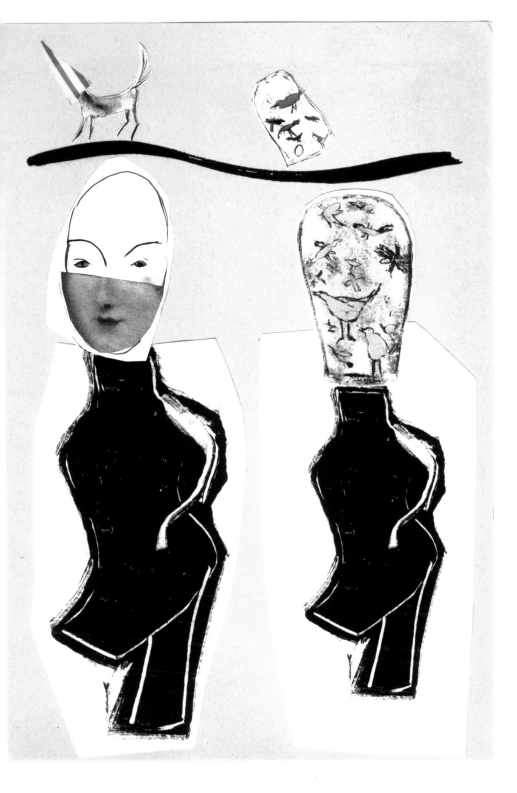

WANt it

From the Pen of
Jock Scot

JOCK RUMINATES ON WHY
HE IS SO CLEVER

I SUPPOSE IQ STANDS FOR INTELLIGENCE QUOTIENT OR SOME SUCH, but that's just an educated guess. I further suppose that you can test yourself on the computer and be given a figure of how brainy you are, according to their system. I was fortunate enough to receive a half-decent schooling 1957–1969 at Musselburgh Grammar School where all the local Protestants, whose parents couldn't afford to have them educated at one of the fee-paying schools "up the toon" in Embra were sent. Really well-off toffs sent their bairns to the residential Boys Public School, Loretto, in Musselburgh itself, but they were a breed apart, in red blazers and short trousers and we used to spit on them when they ventured out of school to the Post Office or a shop. Clever, eh?

But my education and cultivated braininess really began when I reluctantly left school and has continued ever since by simply reading prodigiously. Read, read, read, read, read. I've always done it and continue to do so. I sometimes have six books on the go at once, which, if you are stoned enough, can lead to interesting confusion when you start to get the plots and characters of novels mixed up.

But I usually read factual books, rather than novels, biographies being particular favourites. I must've read six biographies of Nelson, *the* True Great British Hero, and eagerly await the publication of the next one.

George Orwell was the first author to take my fancy and I worked my way through everything he wrote. He was clear, simple and straightforward in his use of language even when dealing with a complex theme. I find Graham Greene similarly easy to read, clear in getting his point over, so have read all *his* books.

The great thing about being a full-on Idler is that you have plenty of time to read and as I refused to get "a proper job" for thirty years, bar the odd bit of roadying, it adds up to quite a few books read. Even when I did have a job, before I wised up and got hip to the Idler trip, I was employed in a library by Embra Corporation and when I wasn't stamping books or chattin' up local 6th formers, I was reading all the latest books. It all mounts up and adds to your all-round brain-iness, even if you are so stoned when reading that you have to go back and read each page again and the next day cannot remember a thing from the text. I'm sure it still all goes in and is logged away somewhere.

As well as the compulsive reading carry-on, there are other ways of exercising the brain muscle (Use it or Lose it): Film and TV for a quick one-two. Although I rarely attend the cinema these days (the last film I saw in a cinema was Almodovar's latest on my birthday over a year ago). My local library punts DVDs for a £1 hire fee, and 'cos there's so much crap on the five channels we receive, I take loads of films out and watch at home with my lovely young wife, in comfort and at our leisure.

Of the telly programmes, my "must see", "never miss it" fave is *University Challenge* and, boy, was I delighted when the *Idler* team trounced *The Economist*, despite my absence from the team, which was carried by master chef, brain box and all-round good guy Rowley Leigh. Fabulous viewing and educational.

Another way I like to exercise the cerebellum is the vanishing art of conversa-tion, the exchange of ideas and opinions verbally with your mates and acquain-tances. But now that I am so brainy, it's become harder to find an equal to converse with. Luckily, my darling young wife is no slouch in the IQ stakes herself. The daughter of a doctor and holder of two degrees, I fell for her one night in the pub as I idly chatted her up, and, feigning interest in her educational history, asked where she studied for her degree. "Which one?" came her brainily immodest showstopper of a reply. I was hooked! Beautiful and brainy!

Listening to popular music has long been a habit of mine, usually when reading, this too can lead to plot and character confusion. It's yet another way of beefing up the brainbox. Wondering what the lyrics mean or why certain words or verses were chosen is endlessly enjoyable fun. No need to list my favourite wordsmiths, but this side of Shakespeare and Dylan you'll do a lot worse than cock an intent ear to the wonderful wordplay of Mark E. Smith of The Fall and young Peter Doherty. You can safely overlook the complete lyrics of Oasis, who are proud of never reading books, and boy does it show in the lyrics to their derivative ditties: "after all / Wonderwall". Give me a break! Captain Beefheart, Don Van Vliet, is my favourite, no question. Others in the Top Ten include Shaun Ryder and Shane MacGowan.

Crosswords are very good for dusting the cobwebs off the brain. I find the most enjoyable one is the *Daily Telegraph* Saturday Weekend Section General Knowledge one. I don't always get more than 2 / 3 of it out, over a weekend and it has become more difficult of late with a new and sadistic compiler, but one day, and soon, I will rip through it and send off my solution, as there is a cash prize and fab dictionary for runners-up, which brings us nicely to another favourite piece of

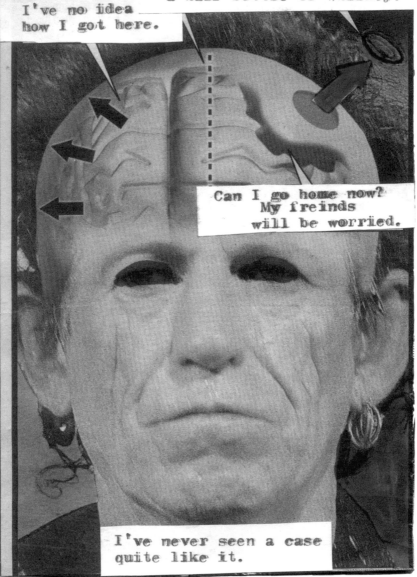

Jock Scot

A Cornucopia of Comedy Loveliness

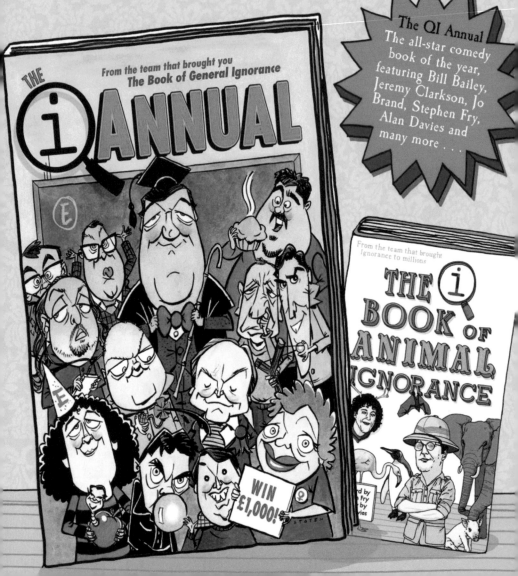

The QI Annual
The all-star comedy book of the year, featuring Bill Bailey, Jeremy Clarkson, Jo Brand, Stephen Fry, Alan Davies and many more . . .

reading material. Yes! Dictionaries. Many a happy hour spent leafing through my over-large collection (another two have just arrived from the OUP).

A bit more before I dash off the illustration which will accompany this piece of fluff. Don't get me wrong, I do not consider myself an intellectual. I just enjoy the thoughts that race through what's left of my once finely-tuned brain. The drugs, booze and a brain haemorrhage have left me feeling as if someone has ransacked the library inside my head, tipping over the shelves and disordering the once correctly, alphabetically arranged books and then kicking them around. All the books are still there, but now they're jumbled up, in a mess. I now sometimes get words, sentences and thoughts mixed up and confused. But, I am aware of the errors I am making soon after I have given voice to them, and have reconciled myself to finding it amusing, when I'm not completely infuriated by my thought or verbal errors. Answers are now often stalled on the tip of my tongue (much to the relief of my Scrabble opponents). But since the dulling and blunting of my once shiny, razor sharp wit and intellect, I find my contemporary peers are relieved that I no longer always have the last word. After all is said and done, no-one likes a clever-dick.

And that's just off the top of my head.

STORIES

One morning, ten years ago, John Lloyd was standing in his tiny cottage in Great Tew wondering what the hell to do with the rest of his life. All of a sudden, with the force on an epiphany, the idea came to him, all-of-a-piece. It was called Quite Interesting (QI for short) and it would be a world-changing project. Flowing from an enormous encyclopaedic database of painstakingly-mined interesting information, it would generate television and radio shows, a series of books, a magazine, an internet community, a string of shops and educational videos. Its long-term aims were to change completely the way we educate children, creating a new school subject and rewriting the National Curriculum; to endow a University Chair of Curiosity; and to create the Royal Quite Interesting Society. It was obviously absurdly ambitious, but it seemed so simple, logical and clear at the time. And so completely real: as if it had all already happened.

"But", thought John, "I really should be getting on with my novel ... " Then, recalling his wife's hilarity — "But you haven't got the intellectual discipline to write a novel!" — he thought, Pooh-Bearishly, that she was probably right and that it that might be rather too difficult to do. "Or perhaps," he thought, cheering himself up, "it's just that I'm not ready yet. I'll get on and do this QI thing while it percolates ... "

A decade later, QI has generated 73 television shows, a six part radio series, four DVDs, a website that gets 300,000 hits a week and three books (with three more in the pipeline), the first of which sold in 25 countries, with 500,000 copies in the UK alone. Admittedly, QI only ever managed to open (and has since closed) one small bookshop but, on the other hand, John has, in fact, just been appointed the world's first Professor of Curiosity, at the University of Buckingham.

The question is: is he ready now to write the novel? You decide. Over the next few pages appear fragments of the book he started but never got round to finishing, offered up like those little windows cut into the hoardings around a building site.

NOTES FOR A BOOK
I CANNOT BE BOTHERED
TO WRITE

by John Lloyd

SIROBIN LOOKED UP FROM HIS DESK.
A man was standing in the doorway, ceremoniously removing his gloves. He was tall, with mutton-chop whiskers and eyebrows that met in the middle.

"Do I have the honour to be in the presence of Sirobin Armstrong?" he inquired.

"That is my name," said Sirobin.

"The Imperial Perfect at Vik," said the man, without further introduction, "has asked me to chair a reporting committee to discover the most important word in the universe."

"Really?" said Sirobin "Why?"

"He wants to give it a prize, "replied the man.

"Ah," said Sirobin. He was not unused to ill-mannered visitors and their peculiar missions. Imperial culture was, as he often said, a broad church.

"A number of candidates suggest themselves," said the man. "But I shall not enumerate them at this juncture, as I have no desire to influence you one way or another in advance of your opinion."

"I see," said Sirobin, gazing at him. "Very gracious of you," he added ironically.

"Would you mind if I removed my trousers?" said the man.

"Not at all, be my guest," replied Sirobin, going back to his work. This was, admittedly, a cultural rarity he had never before experienced in person, but discreetly consulting the Encyclopaedia of Imperial Etiquette on his babbage, as his visitor was engaged in concentrating on his fly-buttons, Sirobin was interested to learn that there were 373 recorded instances of similar practices in the backwaters of Imperial history, and four which were currently extant.

After an improbable amount of heavy breathing, Sirobin heard the man clear his throat, and looked up at him once more.

The man now stood bare-legged in his shirt tails, and Sirobin saw that he had managed to remove his trousers without taking off his shoes, a manoeuvre Sirobin had ceased practising as a schoolboy, and which explained the grunts he had heard earlier. The man's socks were black, Sirobin noted with disapproval — only butlers and undertakers wore black socks — and kept aloft by small elastic suspenders with metal buckles.

"What are your views?" demanded the man.

Sirobin was temporarily taken aback, thinking that he was being asked for his opinion of the man's hosiery, but he checked himself, and in the slight pause that resulted, the man sighed with impatience as if addressing a Dunderhead Seminar or an educationally subnormal baboon.

"Your views, *sir*, on the most important word in the universe. You do have some I assume?" he barked impatiently.

"Indeed, I do", said Sirobin. "Or rather I have one view, which is that there are two candidates that I would place in that category — an equal first as it were — and they are 'and' and 'but'."

The man, his quill hovering over his tomelet, glanced at him sharply.

"This is a serious inquiry, Sirobin", he growled. "An *Imperial* inquiry I might remind you."

Sirobin was not about to be intimidated by empty bluster from a half-naked Icelandic funeral director.

"Oh, but I am serious." he replied animatedly, rising from his chair, "for in these two unregarded syllables resides the whole of known and unknown Truth ... " — the visitor would have inserted "Go on" at this point, but Sirobin gave him no opportunity as he raced across the comma like a homing pigeon over a dovecot-sill — "insofar as 'and' is indicative of the central verity that the universe in all its apparently diverse panoply is, in fact — like the Glorious Imperium itself — All One. 'But' on the other hand is the semiological representative of the Grand Illusion that Nothing Is As It Seems — that there is, in Reality, nothing here but for His Most Tomographical Majesty The Emperor himself, who is both within and without, Blessed and Interminably Repeated be His Name."

"Blessed and Interminably Repeated be His Name," echoed the man formally, sketching the sign of the Gnomon on his breast.

"Ingenious," he said. "Most ... original," he added.

"Not at all. Not at all. Quite the reverse, in fact," said Sirobin, haring off again, like a hare. "It is a very ancient idea. Doubtless you are familiar with 'The Book of But'?" As quickly as he had begun, he stopped without warning and raised an eyebrow.

The man held his gaze for a long while.

"Yes," he said.

He wasn't, which fact was pathetically obvious to Sirobin, in whose estimation the man had now fallen so far that he was down in the sub-basement of his esteem next to the boilers.

"*The Book of But — as you recall,*" interpolated Sirobin pointedly, "is a work of great antiquity, whose authorship is uncertain but is usually ascribed to the MingMong sage Tao Tzu, and it lists, in 42,000 quarto volumes, all the exceptions, contradictions, cavils, opposites and paradoxes that were known in China at that time. It is almost certainly the longest book ever written."

"And *The Book of And?*" inquired the man, casually, looking about as relaxed and intelligent as a boiled lobster.

"What?" said Sirobin.

He was half a million centuries away in the province of Wu, looking up at the Great Shah Gate, on top of which squatted the MingMong sage Tao Tzu, dictating 'buts' through a hollow reed to the blind, ground-based scribe La-Tong.

"What about *The Book of And?*" repeated the man, more uncertainly. He was beginning to blush, lobsterishly.

"*The Book of And?*" asked Sirobin incredulously. "*The Book of And?* Never heard of it. Is there such a book? How could there be? It is a totally absurd notion. What would be the point of it? Now, if you'll excuse me, I have business to attend to,"

"Just testing you," said the man, grinning foolishly.

"What?" said Sirobin again.

The man, though now bright red on all visible surfaces, improbably began sidling across the room towards Sirobin. Whatever many other talents he lacked, impersonating a wide range of crustaceans was certainly not one of them.

"Have you ever seen one of *these* before" said the man, pulling his cock from beneath his shirt-tails and placing it on Sirobin's desk.

Sirobin's eyes flicked down at it. It was long and stout with protuberant veins.

He looked back at the man's face.

"Get out," he said crisply.

"Right," said the man. In a great flurry, he gathered up his trousers and scuttled from the room.

Sirobin pushed back his chair and stretched his legs. Sometimes he wondered, he really did, whether this damned job was worth the candle, dealing as he had to with half the lunatics in the blasted galaxy.

But he sighed briefly, and, dismissing the thought, took up his quill and went back to the task in hand.

It was not till three days later that he noticed that Polypus 42 was nowhere to be found.

❖

"PIPING HOT SNOT, direct from the chef!" shouted the Food Lord, sitting bolt upright in bed. He reached for the dream diary that he kept on his bedside table, scribbled the words in it and went straight back to sleep again.

The Food Lord was an extremely keen and well-organised dreamer. He had long ago realised that his sleeping self was much more creative than his waking self, which was the least useful of what he liked to call his Club of Selves. His waking self, in fact, he had come to think of as merely a kind of major domo — or town crier-self whose only real purpose was to make announcements on behalf on his rather more brilliant selves, as well as, of course to take lunch. The shaving self, the showering self, the golfing self and the driving self all took precedence in this regard, for the waking self, aside from the occasional *bon mot* during meetings, almost never had anything worthy of the name "idea".

The Food Lord had a great deal of respect for ideas, particularly for his own, and particularly when they came to him while fast asleep. In some way, the fact that his waking self had not been responsible for generating them, seemed to make them all the more authentic. Many of VESCO's product lines had been created in this way, and now here he had dreamed another masterstroke.

It had come to him that snot is irresistibly delicious. Everyone likes snot. Digging it out, rolling it into little balls, drinking long strands of it. The Food Lord did not find an insight such as this disgusting. Far from it. If he had been challenged on the matter (not that he had in fact been challenged by anyone on any matter for more than forty years) he would have characterized it as, firstly, refreshingly honest and, secondly, rather brilliantly counter-intuitive. Counter-intuitive was one of his favourite words. The word "disgusting" of the other hand, while not exactly absent from his vocabulary, was used solely with reference to politicians and the contemptible wreckers, blackguards and parasites of the Imperial Health and Safety Authority.

The Food Lord would never, not even in dreams, have dreamt of describing as disgusting anything, whether organic and inorganic, that could conceivably be placed in the human mouth (as well as a considerable number than no sane individual would consider for that role). He had been far too long in the food industry to find physical processes of any kind — death, smells, growths, decay, dismemberment, disease, metamorphosis, bleeding, oozing and suppurating of all varieties — anything other than normal business practice.

The other reason that the Food Lord was blessed with an exceptionally low threshold of disgust was that he was a psychopath, having been brought up single-handedly by one of his father's vending machines. His was a wholly solipsistic universe, in which he (his Club of Selves) was the only "real" person in existence. It had never occurred to him that anyone except himself had feelings of any kind whatsoever. To him, everyone else was merely just another vending machine, or, more commonly, purchasing machine. They had their uses, of course, but the Food Lord had absolutely no regard for their opinions or sensitivities, and indeed privately doubted that they had any.

It is true he maintained a sentimental regard for his old Vending Nanny, and that he was fond of quoting her sagacious gems. "'Stand clear of the doors!' As my old Nanny used to say," he would boom on entering an elevator, opening a drinks cabinet or locking a safe. "Exact money only!" was another treasured aphorism which seemed to be aptly applicable in almost any business situation. But fond of his old Vending Nanny as he was — he had long since retired her to her own cottage on his estate, waited on by three 24-hour maintenance staff — he knew that Nanny was not really a person.

The Food Lord was no fool.

Bastard, yes; fool no.

"... and, if they like it so much, there must be a way of selling it to them!" concluded the Food Lord the following day at VESCO's regular Monday Brainstorming Session.

Everyone felt a strong desire to look at the floor, but no-one did. For a VESCO executive to look at the floor was to commit kareerakiri. It meant you were unable to look the unthinkable in the eye.

"Excuse me, my Lord"

It was young Ferris, the Deputy Questions Manager. The Questions Department was an important section of VESCO Research. It was impossible to think the unthinkable without asking awkward questions.

"Yes, Ferris?"

"A brilliant idea, my Lord".

"That's not a question I hope, Ferris?"

This drew a round of appreciative laughter from the Team. The Food Lord beamed. He looked over his spectacles at Ferris, benevolently. Ferris was the last to stop laughing.

"Marvellous, my Lord, marvellous. Terribly good."

"Glad to be of service, Ferris. And your question is?

Ferris dabbed his eyes-perhaps a mite too theatrically — with a handkerchief.

"Just a minor one, my Lord, pardon my stupidity, but why would people pay to eat their own snot?"

"Good question, Ferris. What do you propose?"

Ferris was caught on the hop, but he knew better than to admit he had no idea. The Food Lord did not suffer people with no ideas gladly.

"My suggestion my Lord is … "

It came to him in a flash.

" … that we apply to ITSA."

The Food Lord frowned.

"The Imperial Trading Standards Authority?"

He cocked his head on one side, like a dugong examining a bookshelf. "Go on," he said.

"We petition ITSA to impose a universal Snot Licence".

The Food Lord raised a questioning eyebrow.

"On Health and Safety grounds. my Lord. It's quite clearly unhygenic to eat un-processed snot. I'm amazed it's still allowed. Anyone in possession of a nose would be obliged to have a Snot Licence, before they are allowed to eat any snot, for which they would have to pay, say, 100 or 150 reals a year."

"I'm with you so far, Ferris."

Ferris warmed to his theme.

"Then, on the same Health and Safety grounds, my Lord, the ITSA would make it a condition that no one may eat unpasteurised snot. We would then collect the snot, pasteurise it, and sell it back to the consumer as say … ah … Vesco Pure Snot Granules or Natural Nasal Broth or… Nummy Nose Candy, say, or a thousand other brands. We could add flavouring, colouring, vitamins or whatever to add *VESCO VALUE*, and I'm pretty sure we could also get the ITSA contract for collecting the Licence fee on the ITSA's behalf."

"Ingenious, Ferris."

Ferris blushed modestly.

"But quite mad."

This brought the house down. The Team laughed with unabashed hilarity. They really meant it this time, out of relief from the release of tension engendered by their revulsion the whole idea and at their fear from the alarming turn the planning meeting had taken.

But Ferris's acting ability had finally met its match. He could manage only a pathetic crumpled smile and his eyes, if they twinkled at all, with twinkling with tears. He was only thirty two, married with two small children, and he did not want to die.

"You see, Ferris, I never proposed that people pay for their own snot."

"Didn't you, my Lord?" stammered the hapless shade. In his mind he was already grey flakes in an urn on Mrs Ferris' mantelpiece.

"No. That would be a fatuous idea, as you have amply demonstrated. A number of insuperable problems suggest themselves."

The Team took up their VESCO pencils and starting taking notes on the VESCO headed notepads before them.

"One. The cost of collecting the raw materials would be astronomical. Two. How would the ITSA police the consumption of illegal unpasteurised snot? Three. Why would we flavour snot, when the point is that it is *already delicious on its own?* But thank you all the same, Ferris, for bringing a bit of … ah … "fun" to the meeting."

The Food Lord now addressed the rest of the Team. He assumed a comical beetle-browed expression of mock despair. "Quite, quite mad," he said, getting another guffaw from his audience. Ferris hung his head in shame, his face an horrible mottled colour like a VESCO Strawberry and Creme Fraiche Fool.

When the merriment had died away, the Food Lord looked serious.

"What I am proposing, ladies and gentlemen," he said, "is that people pay to eat *other people's* snot!"

There was a gasp. The Team rose to their feet as one man and gave the Food Lord a standing ovation. They stamped on the beechwood floor, they cheered him to the rafters. A secretary and two juniors came in from the outer office bearing arm-loads of flowers, and sheaves of congratulatory telegrams from far flung parts of the VESCO Empire were respectfully arranged at the the Food Lord's elbow at the head of the table.

The Food Lord acknowledged the applause graciously, rose to his feet and made demurring gestures, and eventually sat down indicating that the Team should follow suit. They were a damn good Team, he thought to himself — apart from that peculiar Ferris creature.

Hornby-Sturmey, the Questions Manager — and Ferris's immediate boss — raised a discreet finger.

"Yes, QM?" said the Food Lord.

Hornby-Sturmey has a rich, brown, syrupy voice which reminded one of a VESCO Meat-Style Lasagne.

"I wonder, my Lord, if Ferris might be excused?"

"Who?" said the Food Lord.

There were a couple of heavily-concealed smirks, and a snuffly noise.

"Ferris, my Lord?" said Hornby-Sturmey. "He has a conference call in three minutes."

"Yes, yes, yes," said the Food Lord as if waving away a bee. Ferris melted out through the door and was never seen again.

❖

WHAT IS THAT? she asked, pointing at the enormous network of metal that stretched to the horizon.

Ah, said the antiquary, now that, that is very interesting. That, dear lady is a Complete Chinese Typewriter. Very rare indeed. I believe less than a dozen were ever constructed. The problem being that there are fifty thousand characters in written Chinese, so that the key-board (using normal centimetre-wide keys) needs to be a minimum of half a kilometre square. This in itself is only a small part of the problem. One then needs some form of transport system to get around the keyboard, a small golf-cart, say, but if so, obviously the keys will need to be arranged in some form of grid with the keys say a minimum of a metre apart in order to allow access by the cart, which in turn increases the size of the keyboard by a corresponding amount: to, in fact, fifty kilometres to a side. Now, I don't know when the last time was you ever drove a golf cart fifty kilometers, but I have to say, they don't have a lot of poke, most of them do about 25 kilometres a hour. So to type a short phrase in Chinese by this method, where the characters happen by bad luck to be at the extreme edges of the keyboard, as is the case, for instance on this particular model with the words "sweet/and/sour/pork", would take the typist ... (he did some hasty algebra in his head) approximately 22 hours. This is assuming the typist starts from a position adjacent to the first character (in itself rather unlikely) and not allowing for fuel stops. The fuel is the second major problem.

In the first place either the typewriter must be constructed near a garage or one specifically built into or underneath the typewriter itself, otherwise the typist wastes further time driving to the nearest already available garage, and secondly the cost both financially and in terms of the additional time wasted stopping to fill up the tank, visit the lavatory, buy drinks and crisps and so on for one's co-typists are ...

I'm sorry, she said. Sorry to interrupt. Co-typists?

Yes. Co-typists were found to be essential. Two of them. To maximise the available typing time, each typist worked an eight our shift, one doing all the typing and driving, while another one sleeps and the third one map-reads.

Map reads?

Oh, yes. Fiendishly time consuming and difficult skill. The map-reading part is the major difficulty of Chinese typists. After all, practically anyone can drive, and Chinese typing itself is a complete diddle, you just reach out of the window, hit the key with your typing-tong and drive on. But the map-reading takes up the bulk of the nine-year training course. Imagine, you have to memorise the names and meaning of fifty thousand squiggles, many of which are almost identical, and their position not only on the board, but relative to each other. It puts London taxi-drivers to shame, believe me.

The introduction of co-typists, of course, necessarily increases the size of the alleyways between the actual keys to almost double, so that we are now talking about a keyboard very nearly a hundred kilometres square, for which dozens of villages have to be razed to the ground, and thousands of people displaced and re-housed elsewhere.

In addition, in order not to have to increase the size of the fuel tank- with a corresponding increase in the width of the alleyways, it is now necessary to build further garages at convenient points round the edges, with further increases in stoppage time, death from saddle sores of one or more typists, and yet further wastes of time attending their funerals and so forth.

And then there is the problem of where in that enormous network of alleyways dotted with tiny little keys with squiggles on, to put the piece of paper on which the material is to be typed.

It was quickly worked out that having 50,000 huge metal arms up to a hundred kilometres long able to reach to some central point where the paper was situated was clearly neither a engineering, nor an economic possibility, so the solution was, to carry the paper with them, placing it under each key in turn.

Yes, she said, and you say a dozen of these were built?

Well, so they say, said the antiquary, though I doubt it myself.

I'm amazed they built one at all, she said, it's complete madness.

Yes. Madness. But quite interesting madness, don't you think?

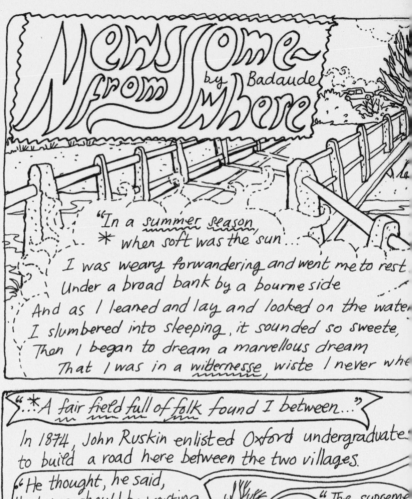

News some from Where
by Badaude

"In a summer season,
* when soft was the sun...

I was weary forwandering and went me to rest
Under a broad bank by a bourne side
And as I leaned and lay and looked on the water
I slumbered into sleeping, it sounded so sweete,
Then I began to dream a marvellous dream
That I was in a wildernesse, wiste I never where

"...* A fair field full of folk found I between..."

In 1874, John Ruskin enlisted Oxford undergraduates to build a road here between the two villages.

"He thought, he said, that we should be working at something that would do good to other people, by which we might show that in all labour there was something noble."

"The supreme accomplishme is to blur the line betwe work an play."

Toyn bee

...each with his own vision of Albion

"The diggers" included Arnold Toynbee and his friend and eventual political opponent, Alfred Milner,...

Milner

I am a British Race patriot!

South Hinksey N W E S North Hinksey
Morning mist or maybe electric static from the local sub-station
blue smoke from the Oxford ring road
"I saw a tower on a tuft, * worthily built, A deep dale beneath, a dungeon therin, with deep ditches and dark, dreadful of sight"
* Piers Plowman by William Langland
Labour, noble? Oscar, when I see a spade, I call it a spade!
When we build let us think that we build forever!
John Ruskin, Slade professor of Art and Social reformer
☆ The Importance of Being Ernest
Oscar Wilde
am glad say that have never seen a spade!☆"
But
"it ended abruptly - in the middle of the swamp. Ruskin going away to Venice, when we came back for the next term there was no leader, and the "diggers"... fell assunder."

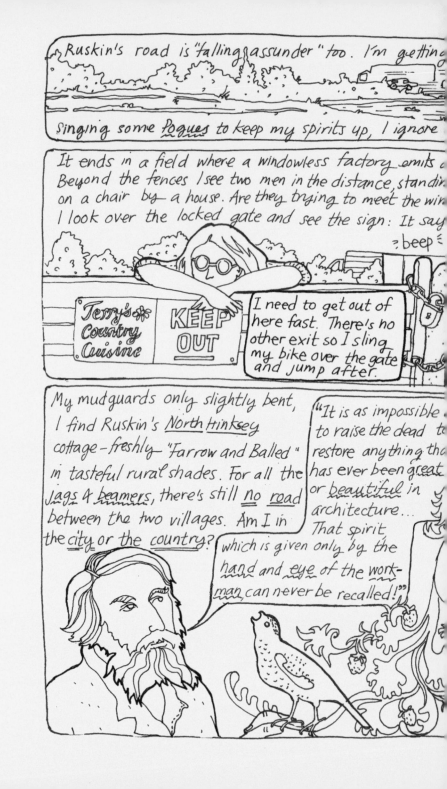

IDLE PURSUITS

How to
LIVE DANGEROUSLY

Warwick Cairns on why danger is safer

¶ Health. Nothing wrong with that, is there? We like health. Safety likewise. And yet, put them together and what do you get? Health and Safety, that's what. And what that seems to mean, these days, is "Don't Take Risks Of Any Kind." It means, don't do this at all; don't do that unless properly supervised; don't do the other until a full risk-assessment has been carried out. It means, amongst other things, make sure your children wear safety-goggles to play conkers. Or better still, don't let them play at all. ¶ But actually, if you really want to be safe, listen to what the Health and Safety people say, by all means — but then go and do the complete opposite. ¶ An example: imagine you have a new job, two miles away, down a busy road. There's no pavement, so you can't walk. But you could cycle, or drive. Cycling, you're eleven times more likely to die in a crash, of head-injuries. So which do you think is safest: drive; cycle wearing a helmet; cycle without a helmet? ¶ Actually, you're wrong. It's precisely the opposite. ¶ Cycling is safest. Without a helmet. You're more likely to die in a crash, of couse, but crashes kill far less people than heart-disease. And if you drive, and don't do exercise to compensate, you're far more likely to die of it. As for helmets, if you're hit by a car, they won't save you. That's not what they're designed for. But they do give you a false sense of security, which means you ride less cautuously. Which means more chance of getting in an accident in the first place. ¶ Another example: children. Do you let them go out to play, with psycho drivers everywhere, and paedophiles lurking on every corner, or keep them "safe" indoors? As it happens, outdoors is safer by far. It would take the average child, outdoors, 25,000 years to be hit by a car. And it would take 186,000 years to be abducted by a stranger. The chances of them having a serious accident indoors are considerably higher. And the chances of them getting fat, and suffering ill health and a reduced life because of it, are pretty much odds-on. ¶ The more you look at things, the more you realise that there is no such thing as a "risk-free" life. Even staying in bed, you have a one in 650 annual chance of being injured by your mattress or pillow. If you go out into the garden, 5,300 people a year are injured by flowerpots. And, in the end, we all die anyway. ¶ In the meantime, in most things, the safest way is often the way that appears, on the face of it, to be the most dangerous. That sounds all wrong, I know; but here's an example — traffic accidents. The way to cut those, you'd think, would be more safety measures — more speed restrictions, more pedestrian safety-barriers, more warning signs. And yet in Holland, in 2003, they ripped the lot out, and made the city of Drachten "Verkeersbordvrij" (free of traffic signs), so people had to think for themselves. Until that time, they'd had an average of eight accidents per year. Since then, there have been none at all. ¶ So if you really want to be safe, the best thing to do is to start ignoring safety advice. ¶ This means developing your own ability to judge and handle risk, rather than expecting others to do it for you. ¶ Start today. Start now. ¶ Sell-by dates? "Traffic lights" to warn you about levels of salt, sugar and fat? How about using your own common-sense instead? ¶ Ditto cycle helmets: they're designed to protect you from a fall, not from being hit by a car, so wear one in the skatepark or on the mountain-bike track, but go bareheaded on the road. Feel your own vulnerability, and learn from it. ¶ Or how about doing something really daring, like letting your children go out to play? Like you did when you were young, in fact, and like children have since the dawn of time. Now that would be brave, wouldn't it. 🌀

Warwick Cairns's new book, How to Live Dangerously, *is published by Macmillan in* Autumn 2008

How to
DIE WELL

The newly-ordained Ru Callendar of the Green Funeral
Company on how he does death differently

¶ "When death comes, like the hungry bear in autumn," as Mary
Oliver put it, it's easy to fuck it up.
¶ You open Yellow Pages, pick up the phone and enter a whole new
world of weirdness in which it is tempting, and very possible, to
duck any real emotional involvement and allow the professionals to
take over. You pick an undertaker, then a vicar, a venue and a coffin.
You find yourself discreetly schooled in bereavement etiquette,
which means not making a fuss and frightening or embarrassing
anyone. You're shown flowers and orders of service. You start to
realise your taste is out of step with what's being offered. Probably
by this time, your only goal is to get through it, but in your haste
to do so you can put yourselves through travesty of ritual, a drab
ceremony that reflects little about the person who has died, and
nothing about those who are left. You've missed the opportunity
and had a McFuneral instead.

It's dull, dangerous and can leave splinters in the heart.

¶ My wife and I are green funeral directors, part of what has been
described as the new funeral movement, and we spend most of our
working life standing in the space between the living and the dead,
trying to explain one to the other. We do everything: dress the
dead, comfort the living, sell the coffin — the curious traditional
mix of councillor and tradesman, but we've taken on another role:
trying to fill the space where the priest used to be.
¶ Officiator is the ugly new term for this, and every funeral needs
one, being some part practical and some part theatre. This suits my
religious inclinations, which aren't godly enough for the Church,
but too much so for the Humanists, somewhere it seems where
most of us stand. I'm the priest you call for when you don't want a

priest. Just try to get me when I'm feeling more like John Wesley than David Koresh. He really raised the bar for all of us with Messianic tendencies. It hasn't happened yet, but if I do bolt the door and start shooting, we'll adjust our bill accordingly.

¶ People think green funerals are about cardboard coffins and joss sticks. Well, yes, green funerals do involve woodland burial sites and wicker coffins, although not exclusively, and we are burdened with that tag, "alternative". At its core, though, the movement is more social than environmental. It's about persuading people to leave behind their half hour slots in a bland crematorium, to stop going to a church if they no longer believe in it and to take to the fields instead. We're swapping municipal waiting rooms and coffee machines for a pile of earth, replacing curtains and crummy sound systems for the sky and a hole in the ground that feels like a wound.

¶ This recipe for emotional disaster is one that millions of us follow. My own experience is that it's possible to sit with this, and the damage it does, for years. But then the next death comes along; as they do, and you find yourself playing emotional catch up. Your grief is out of synch, and that's a problem. If you're lucky, something like the death of Diana happens and you can be part of an outpouring, and do a bit of unexpected grief work. This is what really happened that week, and critics bemoaning our mawkish sentimentality missed it. Keef's right, very few of us met the chick, but the tears we cried that week were real. Mine certainly were — they just weren't for her. Yes, it's grief by proxy, but if we can't act out this stuff through our archetypes what's the point of having them? You'll be asking what pets are for next.

¶ The death and the funeral are really just the beginning, and like most beginnings it encloses the end, so it's important to get it right. Bereavement, especially the first few days is a hallucinatory experience, and when your world goes psychedelic, it's best to have someone by your side who has tripped before. Time slows down. You feel more like giggling than crying. It makes you yawn, perhaps even feel a little horny, as there's nothing like a glimpse of your future end to sharpen the sweetness of now. It might seem outrageous that the sun still shines, that birds tweet fucking tweet and

Richard and Judy bicker on like nothing has happened. It seems impossible that everyone has to go through this; it must be a huge cosmic clerical error. It hurts way too much to be natural.

This is the point where you need to hold steady, don't look away, it's getting real.

This is what we do differently:

¶ We've got rid of the suits, and the euphemisms and we've let go of the bearers.

¶ It means you have to help us carry the coffin, but you are spared four strangers, usually a bit creepy, who stand around looking more upset than you do. Lowering a coffin into the ground is the final act you can do for someone on this earth, and a moment of profound spiritual involvement, so why delegate it? You will thank us for this bit later.

¶ We try to make it less about the car, as modern funerals seem to peak with the arrival of a polished hearse. Great if you're into cars but if not, it's like getting Jeremy Clarkson to organise it.

¶ We let the whole experience sit right in the middle of everything, where it should be. It's as important in your family history as a wedding or a birth, but you don't need to miss supper to feel that. Give yourself enough space. Allow everyone their own reaction. Try to get more time off work than just the day of the funeral. If you handle these days right, then the funeral is more like the credits rolling than the main event. A sort of summing up for those who haven't been through it with you.

¶ By the way, out of all the emotions you will feel, guilt is the least real and the most corrosive. Bin it.

¶ Whatever anyone else tells you, get the children in. It's as much their loss as yours, and they have more to lose if it's handled badly. They can deal with it much better than you anyway.

Prepare to die. Ru Callendar does death differently.

I say it again, get the children in.

¶ We encourage seeing and spending some time with the body, which we don't embalm. The chemicals just aren't worth the risk. We also think there's something psychologically jarring about seeing a dead body looking healthier than you. That is a serious a mixed message. We're not doing this to freak you out but when in shock, knowing something and feeling it are very different things so take a good look at them. They are not sleeping, they really are dead. The more you see this, the sooner you'll be back with the quick.

¶ When it comes to the ceremony we try to keep it simple, and resist the urge to fill up the silences with a New Age pick and mix. Ironically, removing the traditional religious framework can make it feel more religious. Good poetry and music, some talking, some silence, look up, look down, get involved. It's not a performance, something will go wrong and a little bit of low-level anarchy stops it becoming pompous.

¶ Above all we try to be honest. This is not the time to lie. Voltaire said one owes respect to the living, to the dead one owes only the truth. And nowhere is that more true than standing around someone's coffin. Say the unsay able, everyone's thinking it anyway.

¶ When it works, it's living theatre. A proper, useful public ritual that is an initiation into the world of the grown up, but it needs the truth, and to get there you sometimes have to get rid of everything that stands between you and it: the platitudes, the shiny cars, the veneered coffin, everything. Hopefully, what is left at the bottom of the crucible is Love, and nothing but.

¶ Having death as a daily presence keeps you on your existential toes, and I can't pretend we're strangers to the Fear, but the more I see of it, the better it all sits. Weirdly, death can bring out the best in us, and ordinary people have unknown depths of strength and goodness that is thrilling to be around. Human beings are OK, and it's good to have that re affirmed.

¶ Sometimes that's not enough however; so then we rave to Detroit techno all night, what my generation does for fun. It's full of communal release and feels a good ritual opposite to the big sleep. Try it, it's like going to the gym and finding out it's a temple after all.

¶ So I'm taking my ministry seriously. This cultural space needs to be occupied, even if it's squatting. I have no Bishop to please or piss off and no flock to shock. Religion should be about a feeling, an instinctive rising up of the soul and for many, current church practice doesn't do it. I'm not meaning to be offensive or facetious, but I am being called upon to stand around a grave and ask: "what time is love?" This question stands independent of what you believe, and I'm proud to do the asking. When the time comes for you, as it will, I hope you ask it too.

¶ Now everybody stop screaming, get on the floor and be cool. ◉

Gardening
A LITTLE SHED TIME
READING

Graham Burnett on his favourite gardening books

¶ Perhaps one of the most overlooked of garden tools is the book, a perfect companion to the deck chair and a case of fine local ale. By taking time out from the practical tasks of sowing, planting, pruning and mulching we can sit back, contemplate and absorb the wisdom of those who have gone before us and gain not only practical skills but philosophical insights as well. The definitive list of "The Greatest Gardening Books" will always be highly subjective and ultimately pointless, but for what it's worth, here's my contenders for a few 20th century gardening classics ...

Visions
by Clifford Harper

¶ OK, so my first pick isn't actually a book, but so what? It was 1978, a few months after I'd left school, when I discovered Anarchist artist Clifford Harper's utopian *Visions* series of graphics in a little alternative bookshop tucked away in a Brighton back street. The basement walls were decorated with six A3 posters consisting of lovingly detailed line illustrations of what a post-revolutionary society might look like. Depicting community run printing and industrial workshops, solar and wind powered housing estates and publicly controlled radio and TV stations, they were yellowing and dog eared, belonging to an optimistic age of counter-culture that was unfashionable at the pre-dawn of the Thatcher era. But for me they were an epiphany, especially the image of the Collectivised Terrace — an ordinary street in any town or city where the fences dividing previously private and isolated back yards have been torn down, with the resulting open spaces turned into productive plots of vegetables, fruit bushes, chicken houses, cold-frames and bee hives managed by urban farmers and libertarian communards. Thatcher's hardline "there is no such thing as society" agenda was just around the corner and already looming large in the public conciousness. But this was a positive glimpse of how things could be, revealing both the enormous potential of the power of community, and the urban food growing space available by applying just a little common sense, co-operation and imagination to what surrounds us. All it takes is a small shift in our perceptions to see that we all have the power to create better times for ourselves and each other. Maybe this is subversive talk, but who needs supermarkets and agro-chemicals when London alone has some 1.4 million households with gardens, 1388 ha of derelict land, 53,600 ha of protected open space, 14,411 ha of agricultural land plus school playgrounds, rooftops and parks?[1]

¶ *Radical Technology*, the book from which these posters were originally culled, is long out of print, but you can still check out Harper's *Visions* in *Why Work? Arguments For The Leisure Society* published by Freedom Press.

The Allotment – its Landscape and Culture
by David Crouch and Colin Ward

¶ It wasn't until some five years later that I actually got around to some real growing, when the Southend Libertarian and Anarchist Group decided to rent a collective allotment. Debate around the politics of food production — together with a challenge from Ron to stop pontificating and actually DO something — led to about ten of us regularly turning up on the plot in our home-made CRASS teeshirts, mohicans and dreadlocks, empowering ourselves by getting our hands dirty and relearning some of the horticultural skills that earlier generations took for granted. The 'old boys', with their cloth caps, sleeveless jerseys and straight lines of leeks and cabbages, called us the 'coloured haired lot', and our initial contacts with them felt like a culture clash until we realised that we were part of a continuum. These seasoned allotmenteers had for years been putting into practice our anarcho-punk ideals of self-reliance, DIY and mutual aid. Ward and Crouch celebrate this heritage of autonomy and creativity in this classic work first published in 1988. An in-depth survey of the informal relationships between culture, plots and people, it is full of anecdotes and evidence recounting examples that give a sense of that gift economy, community spirit and improvised aesthetic shared by gardeners and growers throughout the ages, right back to Winstanley and the Diggers who in 1649 took the land as a common treasury for all.

The Permaculture Garden
by Graham Bell

¶ I first came across the word "Permaculture" in an article in *Peace News* way back in 1981. The word intrigued me, and I filed it away in some back cupboard of my brain for the next few years. In the meantime I'd acquired an allotment and become a reasonably competent vegetable grower, able to supply my family with plentiful supplies of potatoes, onions, cabbages and beans. I'd also learned much from the books of organic pioneers such as HDRA founder Lawrence D Hills and the late, great Geoff Hamilton. I'd even borrowed David Holmgren and Bill Mollison's *Permaculture One* from the library a couple of times, but found it rather dense and difficult to get my head around. I did however grasp that permaculture had something to do with herb spirals, and decided I'd like one of these in the garden of the house we bought in 1994, after 7 years of being cooped up in a tiny first floor flat. So as I liked the pictures in Graham's book I picked it up in the hope of gaining a few tips. It had nothing about herb spirals, but instead was one of the most eye-opening books I've ever read, changing my whole attitude to gardening, growing and ultimately, life. Giving insights into topics such as soil ecology, water management, composting and energy conservation, Graham gently explains that permaculture is a design system, based around ethics of caring for the earth and each other, and principles of using minimum effort for maximum results, seeing solutions instead of problems and above all, working with nature rather than against, as has been the pattern of most agricultural systems for the last few hundred years. More over, these ethics and principles can be applied to almost any other field of human activity beyond simply growing food: architecture and building to economic systems, forestry management to healthcare, energy production to community build- ing. Somebody once described permaculture as 'revolution disguised as organic gardening', but I think its more important than that. Climate change and peak oil are the earth's way of telling us that we need to alter our behav- iours. With permaculture we can not only make those changes but learn to thrive as well.

The Forest Garden
by Robert Hart

¶ Situated at Wenlock Edge on the Welsh borders, Robert began his forest garden project some forty years ago after observing that a small bed of perennial vegetables and herbs that he had planted up in a corner of his more conventional smallholding was looking after itself with little or no intervention, unlike his annual crops that needed constant attention such as sewing, planting, weeding and so on. Furthermore, these plants provided interesting and unusual additions to the diet, as well as seeming to promote health and vigour in both body and mind.

¶ Noting the maxim of Hippocrates to "make food your medicine and medicine your food", Robert adopted a vegan, 90% raw food diet. He also began to examine the interactions and relationships that take place between plants in natural systems, particularly in woodland. Based on the observation that the natural forest can be divided into distinct layers or "storeys", he developed an existing small orchard into an edible landscape consisting of canopy tall trees, dwarfing fruit trees, shrubs, herbs and climbers, yielding apples, pears, cherries, plums, grapes, gooseberries and currants as well as fresh green salad leaves and herbs as ground cover plants.

¶ His vision was that such low input green and productive landscapes would replace the grey concrete jungles and factory farmed "countrysides" in which so many of us exist; "*Obviously, few of us are in a position to restore the forests. But tens of millions of us have gardens, or access to open spaces such as industrial wastelands, where trees can be planted. and if full advantage can be taken of the potentialities that are available even in heavily built up areas, new 'city forests' can arise . . . "*

¶ To me Robert was a true 20th century hero, whose contribution to our sense of possiblity far, far outstripped the sad, small values my generation have been encouraged to see as aspirational. Robert died in 2000, after which the future of his land fell into doubt. But nonetheless his vision continues to inspire countless numbers who have implemented his ideas in private and community gardens, school grounds, allotments and council estates . . . ◎

NB: figures published 1999 by the SAFE Alliance

Graham Burnett runs permaculture courses and is the author and illustrator of
Permaculture: a Beginners Guide and Earth Writings.
For more information see www.spiralseed.co.uk

Librarium #2

THE AMERICAN NUDIST RESEARCH LIBRARY

Robert Wringham continues his series on remarkable libraries

¶ Perhaps one of the most notable libraries in terms of unusual content is the American Nudist Research Library. With over seven thousand magazines on the topics of naturism and the philosophy of nudity and a copy of almost every book printed on the subject, ANRL is a pretty exhaustive resource. It is based in the Cypress Cove Nudist Resort in Florida and has been around for an impressive twenty-six years. By e-mail, I caught up with the library's president and director, Helen Fisher:

How was the Nudist Library founded?

¶ Twenty six years ago a couple who lived in California (Jayne & Read Schuster) had a collection of nudist/naturist magazines and books which they needed to find space for. They were friends of [the couple] who owned Cypress Cove Nudist Resort. When offered room space, they shipped a huge number of boxes here. A group of Cove residents volunteered to help organize them. From that beginning the collection grew by donations and before long needed more space. A small building was set up for the library and it was staffed, and still is today, completely by volunteers. Eight or nine years ago, having outgrown the building, an addition was made which doubled the building size and which we are now rapidly filling.

Do your librarians go naked while at work?

¶ Ordinarily, the librarians are dressed since we have visiting outsiders who are not members of Cypress Cove and they feel more at ease if we are mostly dressed. The librarians are free to dress as they please. The visiting outsiders make arrangements ahead of their visit so they are admitted through the front gate. They come directly to the library and cannot visit other parts of the park.

How is the library perceived by the locals? There are some who might think your subject matter was a little controversial. Do you get along?

¶ Yes, we are welcomed by the locals. Dean Hadley and Ted Hadley, son and grandson of the resort's owners are members of local town organisations, including the Chamber of Commerce. Once or twice a year, the Chamber visits the Cove for meetings and tours for new members.

Who can access your stuff? Do you have to be a member to get in?

¶ Our materials are available to anyone visiting the library and this includes nudists who are visiting the Cove, although nothing can be taken out of the library. Since everything has been donated and much of the older material is getting fragile, we keep control of handling. Also, we now have about 450 nudist / naturist videos / DVD's which can be watched in the library.

❖

It is how the librarians are described as "mostly dressed" that fascinates me. I wonder if that means you get the occasional naked librarian or that they're all partially naked. Either way, the idea of a Nudist library is marvellous: it is a symbol of how libraries can be relaxed and leisurely places while working to combat censorship and to stand guard over the world's knowledge, no matter how specialised or obscure. ⊚

How to
CREATE THE IDLE HOME
Kevin Telfer on earthships; the bill-free houses of the future

¶ Modern homes in Britain are hard work, ill-suited to idleness. The main reason for homes being like this is that they are extremely expensive to buy, rent and run. This in turn is why so many people need to go out to work: in order to earn enough money to keep up with what looks like a simple enough arrangement of bricks, mortar and glass divided into rooms but is, in fact, financial quicksand. Costs fly in through letterboxes in the form of bills and roll out of bank accounts in the form of direct debits. At the top of the list, of course, is the dreaded but almost ubiquitous *mortgage* (from the old French meaning "pledge to the death") or rent, followed closely by its good friends council tax, electricity bill, gas bill, water bill, TV licence and phone bill. ¶ American eco-architect Mike Reynolds, the inventor of earthships and subject of a new film called *Garbage Warrior*, says that "typical citizens of any developed country are stressed — they're trying to make their mortgage payment or their rent and their utility bill and their car payment." But with the earthship there are no heating bills, no power bills and no water bills. Instead, this is a structure which provides all those functions itself as an integral part of an autonomous and self-sufficient building that does not require connection to centralised utilities. According to Reynolds this means that "life is a lot more mellow — and that's beyond architecture." They're also largely made of old car tyres rammed with earth (hence "earthship"). ¶ The dream of the earthship is this: it is a building that is, without exaggeration, a passport to freedom, where it is not necessary to work to pay utility bills, because there are none. It is a dream of a home that through passive solar warming and ventilation effortlessly heats itself in winter and cools itself in summer, harvests water every time it rains and recycles that same water for multiple uses. Whenever the sun shines and the wind blows, solar panels and wind turbines enable electrical energy to be pumped into the house and stored in batteries. The building looks after its inhabitants and cares for their needs. ¶ The modern-day spin to consumers about ecological living is pitched on one of two sides of the fence — either pay a hefty surcharge for goods and services that are meant to be good for the consumer and the environment, which has led to a feeling, as George Monbiot wrote, that "ethical shopping is just another way of showing how rich you are", or endure green living as some kind of negative primitivism involving terrible hardship. Ecological living through earthships rips this exploitative myth apart: life in them is not about privation or paying "green tax" but about an improvement of the quality of life for its inhabitants at a lesser cost. ¶ This dream sounds idealistic in the extreme, of course, but practical experience has illustrated that it is indeed possible, though there is still the likelihood that a mortgage will be required to finance self-building of an earthship. Nonetheless, earthships have demonstrated that they are extremely efficient in fulfilling the aim of using the natural resources that are immediately available to them. ¶ It is this concept of fundamental thriftiness that gives rise to the idea of conventional houses being like credit cards with large balances that are accumulating debit interest. That "interest" is the utility bills that need paying every month because the home is too inefficient and badly designed to be able to heat itself and provide the electricity and water needed for its inhabitants. By contrast the earthship can be considered as a savings account with the positive interest being the free natural resources that enable the home to function effectively without any costs beyond the initial capital outlay and a little maintenance. ¶ There is also a sense of personal empowerment that earthships give to their occupants — in the most literal sense. The inhabitants of earthships have taken responsibility for generating their own electricity and regulating their own use of it, for ensuring that they have enough water and that all the systems in their building are operating satisfactorily. That responsibility should be seen not in a negative sense; instead the full tools for life and survival are at the occupant's fingertips, a thrilling alternative, surely, to having an account number to quote down the phone to an indifferent call centre operative when something goes wrong. This is also a key strand of eco-psychology — a branch of psychology that suggests that people have become increasingly alienated from the natural environment — the separation, for example, between pressing a light switch and coal being put in a furnace one hundred miles away. According to eco-psychology this alienation is an underlying cause of many psychological problems in developed societies and is a vital factor in the disassociation of human action with consequences on the natural world. ¶ When our very houses, which are meant to be the sanctuary of the idler, make it hard to lead a leisurely life, it is time to start investigating the alternatives. The earthship not only gives its inhabitants more control and opportunity for relaxation but also gives them the satisfaction of knowing that they are having a minimal impact on the environment without having to live by candlelight while bivouacking in the woods. ⦾

Kevin Telfer is the author, with Mischa Hewitt, of Earthships: building a zero carbon future for homes *published by IHS BRE Press, price £25. www.brebookshop.com*

INCREASINGLY
BELEAGUERED
ORDINARY CITIZEN
ONLY HELD TOGETHER
BY TINY MOLECULES.

How to
START YOUR OWN
SCHOOL

Andy Gibson takes education back from the educators

¶ As Thomas Hobbes wrote, "Wisdome is acquired, not by reading of Books, but of Man." Inspired by this idea, I started a school. A free-to-all, unbounded, anarchic, back-of-a-fag packet sort of school. ¶ Back in the mid-Sixties, a group of Stanford students wanted to learn things that Stanford didn't teach, so they started an educational experiment which became known as the Free U — the 'Free University'. It was a noticeboard, on which people posted things they wanted to learn. If enough people wanted to learn something, they ran a class. By the late Sixties the Free U had become the heart of a huge community, with more students than Stanford itself. Some of the Free U's members went on to form the Homebrew Computing Club, from which grew Apple Computers. ¶ In 2006, in London, Soho. An office above Argos. I'd fallen in love with a beautiful Parisian aristocrat (it sounds unlikely) and I needed to learn French, fast. And so, compelled by an adolescent enthusiasm only French girls can inspire, I started a French class in my office. Soon people got the urge to learn other things — guitar, pilates, Spanish, yoga — and they started organising their own classes in the office too. It's still going today. ¶ I discovered that all you need to start a school is an empty room and the right kind of people. The trick is simply to get them to say what they want to learn, and what they can teach. For that, I heartily recommend the humble post-it note. I used this radical anarchist technology to start a school with my fellow students at the School for Social Entrepreneurs, for a total cost of £1.48. I started a free school with a group of peer education enthusiasts, and they produced a crackpot array of subjects from white magic, to dressing like a French girl and even how to fold clothes properly. Now I'm starting Freeschool nights at local pubs and cafes, and helping others do the same.

¶ You would be amazed what the people around you know. People who seem completely dull turn out to be experts in hedgerow gardening, or samurai swords, or pilgrimage. Every day hundreds of years of accumulated knowledge walk straight past us, untapped, and like fools we pour our efforts into learning the same things ourselves when we could just be talking to our neighbours. In the pub. ¶ And so it is time to set the school free. All you need are a few people, some post-it notes and a place to meet. Do it once out of curiosity, or do it regularly with your friends. Start one on the train for your fellow commuters. Start one in your village hall, or your local café, or on the street corner. ¶ Education is far too much fun to be left to the educators. I hope Freeschools can make the world a little smaller and a lot more interesting, and help us learn whatever we want just by sitting in the pub and talking to people. So come on, brave Idlers: go forth and educate!

How to start your own Freeschool night

You need: two colours of post-it notes, some pens and an empty wall.

1. Find a group of people who have some loose thing in common, and meet them in a quiet place which feels like it belongs to everyone. (Pubs are, coincidentally, perfect.)
2. Write the name of your free school on the wall where everyone can see it. (Remember to get the wall-owner's permission.)
3. Tell the community a nice story about how everyone has something to learn, and everyone has something to teach. I use the story of the Free U.
4. Write something you want to learn, and your name, on a post-it note and stick it on the wall under the school name.
5. Explain that one colour of post-it means "I want to learn", the other "I can teach", and pass the post it notes and pens around the group.

6. Have a few drinks and a bit of a chat.
   (This is always a good idea.)
7. Wait for the post-its to start appearing.
   Write some more up yourself.
8. When there are around 50 post-its up there, stand up and teach something yourself. Keep it light, quick and fun, five minutes plus questions.
9. Then ask, "who's next?"
10. Leave the post-its up there, and repeat next week at the same time.

Andy Gibson is putting the Free U ideas online at www.schoolofeverything.com.
He also blogs about the importance of doing things badly at http://sociablism.blogspot.com.
Andy is currently learning behavioural economics, how to write Idler articles and how to cook cabbage. He can probably teach you web technology, radical education theory and innocence, if you buy him a drink first.

GWYN

A DRINK IS FUCKING ACE!

Tea

A FEW OF MY
FAVOURITE TEAS

Elie Godsi stands in for regular tea correspondent Chris Yates
who's gone fishing

¶ Given its ancient Chinese history, Colonial past and the fact that wars and so
much blood has been spilt over it, the humble tea leaf certainly has come a
long way. I still find it bewildering that it has become such a ubiquitous part
of everyday life and for many people, including myself, their drug of choice.
My journey to tea heaven started pretty well at the same point as everyone
else's: a basic bog standard salt of the earth from a bleached bag cup of tea
with sugar. Now from the off let me make it clear I am not a tea snob and
would be happy to drink a good cup of PG or Typhoo if it was offered,
though I've long since dispensed with the need for sugar. It's just that over the
years my continuing journey through a maze of tea plantations has taken me
to so many more interesting places and opened up an unforeseen world of
flavours and sensations that the poor tea bag seems, well, a waste of boiled
water. Most people don't stick to one type of wine and are happy to explore
different grape varieties from different countries and even from different
wine growing regions or estates. To me that humble mass-produced tea bag is
the equivalent of mild mass produced yellow cheese: I can't ever imagine my
world without mature stilton, sharp Lincolnshire poacher, rich creamy feta or
buffalo mozzarella. ¶ Along the way I've sampled various lovely tea bags and
high street tea leaves. Clipper do a wonderful range of black, green and white
teas and their Organic Ceylon and Organic English Breakfast tea bags deserve
specific mention. My dormant taste buds began to tingle with excitement as
hitherto hidden vistas of tea opened up before me, as I reached the delicious
sensuous curves at the end of a flat world. A whole new galaxy of Assam,
Darjeeling and Oolong came hurtling through me as I sipped and slurped
and gulped my way through various tea leaves and tea producing countries.
I travelled the tea world in a mug. ¶ Then in a moment of epiphany I found
what I was looking for. Single estate Ceylon tea from Sri Lanka. Only not just
one estate, but a whole array of different estates from different regions, each

with their own altitudes, wet seasons, prevailing winds, growing methods and picking seasons. Kandy, Nawara Eliya, Morawak Korale districts all promised and delivered. Then I found Dimbula, one of the first areas to be planted after tea took over from coffee in Ceylon in the 1870s on the extensive western slopes of the tea planting districts, with a range of teas from full bodied flavour to light, delicate and fragrant. Then higher up the Uva district on the eastern slopes of Sri Lanka's central mountains teas with distinctive flavour and pungency. I had found my tea heaven: Orange Pekoe was the "one", the tea for me. Orange refers to the colour of the tea, ranging from light copper to deep red. Pekoe comes from the Chinese "Pak Ho", referring to the "white hair" after the hairs found on the underside of the best leaves. ¶ So now back to practical reality. My favourite tea dealer at the moment is the wonderful Imperial Tea's that can be found at www.imperialteas.co.uk. There you will find the world's rarest tea Jun Shan Silver Needles from China at £1000 per kg: it is picked on just one morning of the year and the whole harvest weighs around 50 to 100lbs! But here are a list of my favourites, all at far more reasonable prices, all of which I keep and brew according to my needs and tastes: Dotel Oya from Kandy district is subtle but strong in flavour, usually my first cup of the day; and from the Dimbula district, the assertive but refined Blackwood Organic, the almost perfumed Waulugalla, the dependable Ruhunu as well as the delicious and aptly named "precious jewel". ¶ Unless I'm in large company I can't be bothered with tea pots. Imperial Teas sell a range of infusers and my favourite is made from wire gauze with a delicate little bamboo handle. It sits perfectly on the rim of my Denby curved mug and is wide enough and deep enough to let the leaves breathe and swell to their full flavour delivering best. I wait a few minutes until the leaves have unfurled and regained their green tinge. Simply lift the infuser and the tea is ready to be drunk as you like it — I prefer mine with a little milk, but take time to admire the different colours of the tea first (white inside the mug helps), something that in itself lifts my spirit before I've even taken the first sip. If your tap water tastes poor make sure to filter it first, it really does make a huge difference. ¶ Enjoy! ☻

Angling
GREAT SNAKES

Kevin Parr on the sad decline of the mysterious eel

¶ My early fishing experiences were based almost entirely at sea. My father had grown up on the Dorset Coast and knew the rocks and crags well, so with my brother and I at an inquisitive age, rod bags were dusted off, hooks sharpened and my father's own fishing fire rekindled. Soon the rod bag was an essential part of the holiday luggage, though as our holiday locations were always in the wilds of the west — the moors of Devon, Snowdonian and Cumbrian mountains and the Western Isles of Scotland — fishing opportunities were somewhat limited. Tumbling mountain streams are great fun to play in, the water runs clear and cold and responds particularly well to damming, but there just aren't any fish in them. ¶ Or so we thought. ¶ One unusually warm afternoon in the foothills of Snowdon was spent on the banks of a lively rivulet which tumbled out of the mountains and into the valley where we met it. Beneath a small bridge was formed a deep pool, perhaps five or six feet, where us kids could swim while our parents read newspapers and enjoyed the sunshine. I had spotted a couple of small trout darting downstream, but we swam all afternoon, blissfully unaware of what was lurking beneath the boulders. ¶ As the sun set, they revealed themselves. Eels. Great, menacing snakes, emerging from lairs between the very rocks which our toes had been touching just minutes earlier. We saw, perhaps, a dozen and I was transfixed. They seemed enormous to an eight-year old and so unlikely. What could they eat and where had they come from? ¶ Eels, however, are great scavengers, and, when the need arises, handy hunters as well. Their tastes are certainly catholic, and the fisherman has traditionally caught them on all manner of baits. Recent history, however has witnessed a change in fortune for *Anguilla anguilla*, the European Eel. I may not have known at the time, but those fish in the Welsh stream were far older than I, and had travelled many miles further. ¶ It is astonishing that so little is known about such a familiar species, but much of the accepted eel lifecycle is conjecture. It is widely believed, and almost certainly true, that the freshwater eel breeds in the Sargasso Sea in the Caribbean, whereafter the larvae follow the Gulf Stream back across the Atlantic and make their way into the fresh waters of Europe. Elvers, immature eels, have been harvested for centuries as they enter our estuaries. Caught in nets as they head upstream, and then flash-fried in bacon fat, there seemed to be an endless and tasty bounty for many. The elvers have all but disappeared, however, and nobody is absolutely sure why. A nematode worm, a parasite that lives in the gut, has arrived from the far east and has certainly been to blame for much of the eels' plight. Over-fishing and a shift north of the gulf stream are also viable population checks, but estimates of a 99% reduction in population of the eel presents a tale which can surely have but a sorry end. ¶ That we know so little about this species, is also one of the reasons why its demise is so tragic. Aside from the lack of scientific knowledge regarding it's reproduction, we also know so little about the eel's actual life. ¶ Having found freshwater, it doesn't simply find a lair for a year or two before heading back out to sea to breed. Some eels just keep exploring, and some grow very old and very, very large. ¶ It is believed that on damp, wet nights eels can actually travel overland to find new habitat. A belief based on the fact that there is not an unpolluted waterway or landlocked pond in Britain that has not now, or at some point, sustained a population of eels. What is more likely, is that the elver, being so small, may find its way underground along spring-fed, sub-terraneal water tracts, or, indeed, they may be caught, carried, and then dropped by predatory birds, or introduced by way of human intervention. What is absolutely certain, though, is that no one can be sure as to just how great an age an eel may reach. For whatever reason, and it is fair to assume that they simply can't get there, some eels do not ever leave freshwater to head back to the Sargasso. Instead they settle back and attain gargantua. ¶ The British record eel is over eleven pounds, but I have seen one far, far bigger. ¶ Fishing an ancient and favourite pond in my mid-teens, a bright day was leading to little action. I climbed a tree to look across the water and, some 200 yards away, spotted a big pike making its way towards me. I watched it as it came closer and got bigger — the breadth of the fish suggested I was looking at a pike of maybe twenty pounds, but something didn't quite fit. ¶ As it swam beneath me, its back proud of the water, I can vividly recall my stomach cartwheeling. It was an eel. It was at least five feet long, and as wide as the span of my hand. I was utterly dumbstruck, and couldn't fish for the rest of the day. ¶ Bigger eels than mine certainly exist, however. Not least in Loch Ness. Underwater surveys in the Loch have revealed amazing amounts of eels with individuals estimated at six feet in

Know your **A**sp from your **E**lephant

From the team that brought Ignorance to millions

THE ⓘ BOOK OF ANIMAL IGNORANCE

Foreword by
Stephen Fry
Forepaw by
Alan Davies

ff

QI.COM

length. Locals have suggested they grow far bigger, and a specimen found trapped at Foyers Power Station on the south-eastern shore of Ness, was rumoured to measure in excess of ten feet. ¶ To put an age to such a fish would be all but impossible, but for a cold-blooded creature to grow to even four feet in the cold depths of a Scottish loch would surely take many, many decades. ¶ The fact that eels enjoy such longevity could also be their downfall. These fish still terrorising the depths of our inland waters are not ever going to reproduce, and whatever is causing the demise of the elvers may be too late to remedy. ¶ So should you catch an eel or simply see one, give a moment's thought, for there may not be many left to be jellied in a jar. 🐚

The Idler *Abroad*

PERFECT NOTHINGNESS

Chris Moss visits the Patagonia of explorer WH Hudson,
and finds peace in the emptiness

¶ "At last, Patagonia! How often had I pictured in imagination, wishing with
an intense longing to visit this solitary wilderness, resting far off in its primitive and desolate peace, untouched by man, remote from civilisation! There it
lay full in sight before me — the unmarred desert that wakes strange feelings
in us; the ancient habitation of giants, whose foot-prints seen on the sea-
shore amazed Magellan and his men, and won for it the name of Patagonia."
¶ So begins the narrative of William Henry Hudson's *Idle Days in Patagonia*
(1893), about his sojourn to the Río Negro in southern Argentina in 1870. As
for all travellers of his era Patagonia already existed for Hudson as a mythical,
magical landscape. After a rough sea voyage down the Atlantic coast, he was
expressing relief at arriving — but he was also celebrating having made a
long-cherished dream come true.
¶ Born in Quilmes, on the fertile pampas just south of Buenos Aires, Hudson
had always loved the countryside, especially riding, birding and sipping *yerba
mate* tea with the gauchos. He travelled to Patagonia to do all these away from
the clutter of family and friends and, at the same time, to make a record of
the region's natural history for a British scientific society.
¶ But this plan was dashed shortly after arriving. Hudson recalls in the second
chapter, "How I became an Idler", how an accident led to his being obliged
to take Patagonia lying down:

> At length, one hot afternoon, we were sitting on our rugs on the clay floor
> of the hut, talking of our journey on the morrow, and of the better fare
> and other delights we should find at the end of the day at the house of an
> English settler we were going to visit. While talking [with a local rancher] I
> took up his revolver to examine it for the first time, and he had just begun
> to tell me that it was a revolver with a peculiar character of its own, and
> with idiosyncrasies, one of which was that the slightest touch, or even
> vibration of the air, would cause it to go off when on the cock — he was
> just telling me this, when off it went with a terrible bang and sent a
> conical bullet into my left knee, an inch or so beneath the knee-cap.

The Andes near Trevelin, a town settled by the Welsh colonists. That tufty grass, called coiron, is typical of the steppe.

A Patagonian gaucho, taken near El Calafate.

The pain was not much, the sensation resembling that caused by a smart blow on the knee; but on attempting to get up I fell back. I could not stand. Then the blood began to flow in a thin but continuous stream from the round symmetrical bore which seemed to go straight into the bone of the joint, and nothing that we could do would serve to stop it. Here we were in a pretty fix!

Hudson writes that, after the initial pain and hassle, he gave himself over to 'some of the happiest moments of my life'. For several weeks he had to rest and allow his wound to heal. Staring at the ceiling or lounging in the garden of a lonely ranch, Patagonia's horizons became even wider.

¶ Four decades earlier a very young Charles Darwin had travelled through Patagonia while accompanying Robert FitzRoy on his famous surveying expedition. Hudson was stirred by something he had read in the scientist's 1839 *Journal of Researches* (aka *The Voyage of the Beagle*): "In calling up images of the past, I find the plains of Patagonia most frequently cross before my eyes," wrote Darwin. "Yet these plains are pronounced by all most wretched & useless. They are only characterized by negative possessions:– without habitations, without water, without trees, without mountains, they support merely a few dwarf plants. Why then, and the case is not peculiar to myself, do these arid wastes take so firm possession of the memory?"

The empty road is at a ranch on the cliffs south of Trelew, another Welsh town.

¶ Hudson takes up where Darwin left off and seizes upon this seeming negativity, coming to a gradual realisation that the essential state of the human mind is echoed by the bleak, morbid, inchoate landscape. On seeing Patagonia, man sees his soul reflected, he argues. "The grey, monotonous solitude woke other and deeper feelings, and in that mental state the scene was indelibly impressed on the mind." The dun-coloured plains, in not arousing wonder or surprise, allow the soul to meditate and look in upon itself.

¶ Hudson argues that this correspondence of the mind with its surroundings endures long after one's travels. While jungles, beaches and busy landscapes only come back to us vaguely, he says, Patagonia is remembered "so complete in all its vast extent, with all its details clearly outlines". Less is more; less is a means of accessing the Sublime.

¶ The *nada* — the perfect nothingness — of Patagonia gets to people in different ways.

¶ Spanish *conquistadores*, on finding no silver mines, thought it a waste of space. Darwin noted its "tame sterility" with a sort of perturbed fascination. More recently, Bruce Chatwin recorded meeting expat ranchers who were driven to madness by the desolation and turned to drink. Chatwin himself chattered his way round the region, thrusting himself into the vast library of Patagonia literature to give the weirdness and solitude of the steppe some meaning, and told the readers of his masterful travelogue In Patagonia (1977) to keep busy by walking.

¶ For Hudson, however, Patagonia is the ultimate landscape of calm reflection, and a powerful stimulant to the imagination. He found the bland emptiness, the absence of human of settlement, and the formless, void aspect of the place to be a keen reminder of mortality. Where Darwin had rummaged for fossils, he visited the tombs of the Tehuelche Indians and looked inside the skulls of their half-buried forbears.

> To go back for a brief space to those Golgothas that I frequently visited in the valley, not as collector nor archaeologist, and in no scientific spirit, but only, as it seemed, to indulge in mournful thoughts. If by looking into the empty cavity of one of those broken unburied skulls I had been able to see, as in a magic glass, an image of the world as it once existed in the living brain, what should I have seen? Such a question would not and could not, I imagine, be suggested by the sight of a bleached broken human skull in any other region; but in Patagonia it does not seem grotesque, nor merely idle, nor quite fanciful.

¶ Hudson looks out at the world through the eye-sockets of the skull and tries to re-imagine Patagonia as it would have appeared to a native:

> In the cavity, extending from side to side, there would have appeared a band of colour; its margins grey, growing fainter and bluer outwardly, and finally fading into nothing; between the grey edges the band would be green; and along this green middle band, not always keeping to the centre, there would appear a sinuous shiny line, like a serpent with glittering skin lying at rest on the grass. For the river must have been to the aboriginal inhabitants of the valley the one great central unforgettable fact in nature and man's life.

¶ Hudson searches for the purity of the aboriginal vision of the Río Negro and its grey banks. Today's travellers can do the same. In the foothills of the Fitz Roy range, right down at the southern tip of the Andes, I saw dead trees piled up like dry bones, lying on an inland beach left behind when the waters receded tens of million of years ago. Dinosaur-bibbers love to come to the Patagonian steppe because nothing ever changed there; in some areas there are even giant footprints left behind in the caked mud.

¶ Hudson's Idle Days in Patagonia is an invitation to seek in these dead things something essential about life: "If I should have a reader ... who has felt the

CALODROMAS ELEGANS

DOLICHOTIS PATAGONICA

On the plate: the bird at the top (calodromas elegans) is the crested tinamou and the lower one is the Patagonian mara, a kind of cavy (like a guinea pig, but big).

The famous Old Patagonian Express, early 1990s.

mystery and glory of life overcoming his soul with wonder and desire, and who bears in his system the canker of consumption which threatens to darken the vision prematurely — to such a one I say, TRY PATAGONIA. It is far to travel, and in place of the smoothness of Madeira there would be roughness; but how far men go, into what rough places, in search of rubies and ingots of gold; and life is more than these".

¶ The capitals are Hudson's. Like Chatwin, he wanted his readers — among the most avid were Conrad, Ford Madox Ford and George Gissing — to turn to nature for the good of their health. But rather than stomping all over the place and hopping from town to town in search of some meaningful anecdote or encounter, Hudson exhorts us to luxuriate in infinite gloom and to learn how to travel without moving. Like a Taoist monk, Argentina's mystical twitcher does not do this to give us an overdose of sadness, but because he thinks we'll find an obscure but profound peace and pleasure in the emptiness. ☺

Chris Moss is the author of Landscapes of the Imagination: Patagonia (Signal Books), published in March 2008.

Photographs © Chris Moss

Finally, the bird running away on the road is a choique or Lesser Rhea (the variety we see down in Patagonia).

number9dream — DAVID MITCHELL — SCEPTRE

HENRY JAMES — The Turn of the Screw and The Aspern Papers

Muriel Spark — The Prime of Miss Jean Brodie — PENGUIN CLASSICS

THE NIBELUNGENLIED — PENGUIN CLASSICS

The Valley of Fear — Sir Arthur Conan Doyle

CONAN DOYLE · A STUDY IN SCARLET

SIR ARTHUR CONAN DOYLE — A Study in Scarlet

SIR ARTHUR CONAN DOYLE — The Memoirs of Sherlock Holmes

Sir Arthur Conan Doyle — The Uncollected Sherlock Holmes

A Study in Scarlet · Sir Arthur Conan Doyle

NIETZSCHE — The Birth of Tragedy

NEUROMANCER — William gibson — PENGUIN CLASSICS

William Shakespeare — HAMLET

NEVER-ENDING DAYS OF BEING DEAD — Chad Taylor — MARCUS CHOWN

ELECTRIC

HOPKINS | THE MAJOR WORKS — OXFORD

Mudge

Night Train — MARTIN AMIS

ARTHUR MILLER — Death of a Salesman

DAVID MITCHELL — number9dream

RADCLIFFE | THE MYSTERIES OF UDOLPHO — OXFORD

When Flesh Becomes Word

LAURENCE STERNE — The Life and Opinions of Tristram Shandy, Gentleman — PENGUIN CLASSICS

ZEN FLESH, ZEN BONES — COMPILED BY PAUL REPS

LEO TOLSTOY — Anna Karenina — PENGUIN CLASSICS

ROUSSEAU — LA NOUVELLE HÉLOÏSE — JULIE OR THE NEW ELOISE — PENN STATE

KITCHER SCHACHT — Finding an Ending — REFLECTIONS ON WAGNER'S RING — OXFORD

THE VOYNICH MANUSCRIPT — & ROB CHURCHILL

Books

BUSMAN'S HOLIDAY

¶ Jennifer Bornstein's *How to Ride the Bus* (published by new art publisher Four Corners Books, £6.95) is a welcome reminder of the oft-noted idle pleasures of bus travel. Conscious however that someone's got to drive the thing, she prefaces her meditation on favoured New York bus routes, with dignified portraits of the drivers on their breaks. Don't forget that, like working for the post office, driving a bus is a job often favoured by artists, writers and musicians who are trying to scrape a crust. So next time you flash your oyster card or bus pass, try being friendly to the men and women who make this classic urban pleasure possible. ⊙

Books

FASTER, HIGHER, STRONGER

The tyranny of the Olympian ideal and a portrait of childhood in Georges Perec's W, writes James Bridle

¶ The Frenchman Pierre Frédy, Baron de Coubertin, founder of the modern Olympics, believed that the Olympic games could be a force for peace in the world, creating a new religion "adhering to an ideal of a higher life, to strive for perfection", as well an an élite "whose origins are completely egalitarian". But they had a darker, parallel root: Coubertin had seen his nation humiliated in the Franco-Prussian war of 1870—71 and blamed its failure on the dissoluteness of its youth. Only through strenuous physical exercise could the fortunes of the state and the cult of the victor be restored.

¶ This tension has long manifested itself in the Games themselves, a time-honoured venue for controversy, international point-scoring and revenge. Following Hitler's politicisation of the games in 1936, the first boycotts occurred in 1956, in response to the twin crises of Suez and Hungary. More followed in 1972 and 1976, as African nations protested against the racist systems of Rhodesia and South Africa, and most famously in 1980 and 1984 as the Cold War giants took turns to snub each other at the starting line.

¶ The Black September action in Munich, 1976, is the most famous attack on the Olympic ideal, but to this day Iranian athletes are forbidden to compete against those from Israel, while periodic wranglings between China and Taiwan have seen both restrict their presence at the games. And all this without the ongoing doping scandals (although it should be noted that the first doping disqualification in Olympic history was for the use of alcohol: the Swede, Hans-Gunnar Liljenwall, whose "two beers" to calm his nerves before the 1968 pentathlon led to the wholesale exclusion of the Swedish men's team).

¶ Coubertin himself believed that art was an essential component of the Olympic ideal: "In the heyday of Olympia the glory of the Olympic Games consisted of a harmonious blending of arts and sports. So it should be once again in the future." From 1912 to 1948 artists too could compete in the games, receiving medals for submissions in the categories of architecture, literature, painting, sculpture, and music (the latter, somewhat bizarrely, only submitted on paper) — providing the artworks themselves were inspired by sport.

¶ It is difficult to argue that Georges Perec's 1975 novel, *W, or The Memory of Childhood*, takes as its central image the resonant Games: the Games themselves (including the Spartakiads, held first by the Soviet Union in opposition to the "bourgeois" Olympics, and later as a companion, wholly communist competition); the Olympic villages; the striation of society into organisers; the corps of judges and referees; the body of the athletes and the mere spectators; and the succession of trials, heats and finals that lead to that most exclusive of platforms: the podium.

¶ *W* is a dual narrative, an evocation of the writer's childhood and a description of the island of W, somewhere in the South Pacific, in the inhospitable reaches of Tierra del Fuego. On W, obscure of origin but "almost exclusively Aryan" in population, "Sport is king."

¶ The active inhabitants of *W* — that is, the sportsmen, and the trainers, managers, dieticians and so on necessary to their endeavours — are concentrated in four villages which compete against one another according to a fixed schedule, culminating in annual Olympiads at which the fate of the villages — their reputations, their food supplies, even the names of the inhabitants, are decided. More regular trials are held within the villages, and less vicious but no less significant championships are contested between neighbouring villages.

¶ Perec worked for many years as an archivist in the Neurophysiological Research Laboratory attached to the Hôpital Saint-Antoine in Paris. The daily drudgery of his work, the handling of vast tracts of data, charts and figures, infected his writing. His most famous novel, *Life: A User's Manual*, is filled with the minutiae of lists, inventories and accounts: the classification of life into comprehensible, actionable cells. In the obsessive training, timing and ranking of the Olympic athletes, and the consequent exclusion of the weak, lame and just not good enough, he saw the racial categorisations, the skull measurements and train timetables, that underpinned the great tragedy of his life and of the twentieth century.

¶ At the start of *W*, the writer notes: "I have no childhood memories. Up to my twelfth year or thereabouts, my story comes to barely a couple of lines: I lost my father at four, my mother at six; I spent the war at Villard-de-Lans. In 1945, my father's sister and her husband adopted me." Perec's father Judko Peretz, an emigrant from Poland, was killed fighting for France in 1940. His mother Cyrla perished in Auschwitz.

¶ *W* is a tale told by a child narrator, with only occasional interjections from an elder, and those serve only to remind us that such recollections are at best fragmentary, and flawed. What remains is an outline — of a coastline, of a political system, of a series of events that together add up to an obliteration. In *La disparition* (translated into English as "A Void") Perec writes an entire novel without the letter "e": this omission provides the block on which his characters stumble and lose themselves, forever aware that history is only experien-

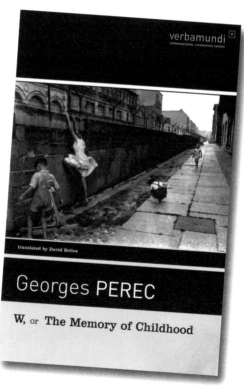

tial, it can not be retold.

¶ War itself provides the narrative that obliterates the individual experience. As the athletes of *W* are subsumed in the Olympian ideal, so the victims of war, both direct and indirect, lose not only their lives but their names and histories. *W* is a challenge to the past to see the Holocaust as it occurred; and a challenge to us to see through the murderous rhetoric and actions of our own time. In *W*, everyone is complicit. ◉

Books: QI recommends
A READING LIST

The Oxford English Dictionary

The greatest reference work in the English language, it's 300,000 or so entries are now available online. In 1884, James Murray planned it as a four-volume, 6,400 page, ten years project. Five years later, they had only got as far as 'ant'. The 3rd edition, due in 2037, will be over 40,000 pages long.

Encyclopedia Britannica 11th Edition (1911)

The last great encyclopedia to be written by real people — from Einstein and Ernest Rutherford, to Bertrand Russell, Swinburne and the anarchist Kroptokin. Bigger, deeper, better written and full of astonishing lost knowledge.

Cassell's Dictionary of Slang
Jonathan Green

The work of a single human being, Green's book goes further and wider than any other record of slang and manages to combine unimpeachable historical scholarship with the appropriate wit and raciness (e.g. 'gooseberry bush' was a 19th century euphemism for pubic hair). The OED of the street.

The Oxford Companion to Food
Alan Davidson

In the grand tradition of reference books as lifetime obsession, this, the work of thirty years, is also written with warmth and an irresistible humour. It's a book to get lost in: to dawdle over, to savour. The history and science of refrigeration, the sex life of eels, how to butcher a reindeer: it's all in here.

Collins New Naturalist Series

100 volumes have been published in this matchless series since 1945, the most recent being Oliver Rackham's masterpiece, *Woodlands*. Collectible, beautiful, conceived "to interest the general reader in the wild life of Britain by recapturing the inquiring spirit of the old naturalists." Need we say more.

England in Particular
Sue Clifford & Angela King
An amazing gazeeter of all thngs English, from trees, rivers, and apple varieties to mummers plays, spotted dick and the 10,000 mile Sustrans cycle network. Produced by Common Ground, an empowering celebration of the commonplace, the local, the vernacular and the distinctive.

Flora Britannica
Richard Mabey
The simplicity of the concept (to describe all the UK's flowers, plants and trees and their cultural significance) doesn't begin to communicate the richness within. Also produced in conjunction with Common Ground, it tells us as much about ourselves as plants. Keep it by the bedside: you'll never look at a hawthorn bush in the same way again.

A Natural History of the Senses
Diane Ackerman
An examination of each of our five senses to tell the history of our species. Whether she's explaining why the Empress Josephine used violet perfume, exploring or craving for chocolate or describing the launch of a space shuttle, Ackerman changes the way we see, hear, feel and taste the world.

Nature's Building Blocks
John Elmsley
Elmsley's mini-encyclopedia is an endlessly compelling tour of the periodic table. Did you know that antimony killed Mozart, that the inert gas xenon is used as the main fuel for spaceflight or that the small Swedish village of Yttersby yielded four new elements? Scholarship stuffed full of wonder.

Brewer's Rogues, Villains & Eccentrics
Willie Donaldson
The inventor of Henry Root's essential work of historical biography that just happens to be the best loo book of all time. Next to "Mad Jack" Mytton the wildest modern sleb excesses appear rather tame and where else would you learn that Alistair Crowley designed boomerangs as a hobby?

What It Means To Be 98% Chimpanzee
Jonathan Marks

A brilliant, controversial polemic, which savages the soft underbelly of evolutionary psychology. What does it mean? Not much more than being 40% daffodil. Modern popular science at its best.

The Man Who Knew Infinity: A Life of the Genius Ramanujan
Robert Kanigel

Ramanujan was a mathematical genius who lived too much of his too short life in poverty working as an office clerk. His 3,900 separate discoveries, which continue to influence maths and physics were balanced by a deep spiritual integrity. Uplifting and humbling: the opposite of a misery memoir.

Labyrinths of Reason
William Poundstone

Subtitled "Paradoxes, Puzzles and the Frailty of Knowledge", this is a profound and endlessly fascinating collection of philosophical experiments. Poundstone is a Sceptic in the richest sense of the term and whether he's writing on Sherlock Holmes or parallel worlds, his writing remains sparklingly clear and accessible. Dental floss for the brain.

Thought As A System
David Bohm

Bohm was a leading quantum physicist and worked on the Manhattan project. He became a close friend of the Indian philosopher Krishnamurti and this book is a record of Bohm's seminars where he reviewed their work together. It is a visionary meeting of East and West and of philosophy with spirituality and politics. Anyone who worries about our future needs to read it.

The Book — On The Taboo Against Knowing Who You Are
Alan Watts

A short, profoud book by one he most urbane and approachable of modern mystics, drawing on Hinduism, Chinese philosophy, pantheism, and modern science to remind us we are all 'God in disguise'.

Catching the Light: The Entwined History of Light and Mind
Arthur Zajonc

A history of light by a quantum physicist who hangs out with the Dalai Lama. As thoughtful, informative and irresistible as it sounds.

The Field: The Quest For The Secret Force of the Universe
Lynne McTaggart

This may sound like a "woo-woo" book, but in fact it s a tough-minded tour d'horizon of the outer limits of modern physics. The idea of the universe as a single, vibrating, quantum field will one day be mainstream. You read it here first.

The Tractenberg Speed System of Basic Mathematics
Translated by Ann Cutler and Rudolph McShane

Can't do maths? Read this and you'll soon be able to do high-speed calculations of unexpected complexity. Not only is this a great brain workout, but as the maths-fear dissipates, the mystery of numbers — the secret language of the universe — will deepen.

Drawing on the Right Side of the Brain
Betty Edwards

For twenty years this book has been quietly teaching people, still terrorised by their memories of school art classes, that they can draw. It is clear, un-patronising and in the space of a day the results are remarkable. Nobody ever regrets learning to draw. A classic that actually does change your life for the better.

The Art of Looking Sideways
Alan Fletcher

Alan Fletcher was one of Britain's greatest graphic designers. This, his visual diary, is a modern classic. It is a great slab of a book and a constant source of inspiration, jemmied full of anecdotes quotes, paintings, photographs and found objects. It's as refreshing as a visit to the best art gallery or museum. 🌀

Music

BEAUTIFUL AND ANARCHIC
AND CRAZY AND GREAT

Idler literary editor Tony White interviews Mark Eitzel
of American Music Club

MARK EITZEL HAS BEEN MAKING RECORDS AND PERFORMING WITH
American Music Club since the mid-1980s. The string of albums that have
seen him called "America's Greatest Living Lyricist" include *California*,
Everclear and this year's *Golden Age*. Start anywhere you want and you'll find
plaintive, witty songs that have been bracketed as alt.country, americana,
and indie, amongst other things, but which exceed attempts at categorisa-
tion. What there is is a cussed and contrary artistic streak and an illuminat-
ing honesty and insight into human dramas — from the out-and-out elegaic
(as in *Everclear's* 'Why Won't You Stay') to, say, a moment of fragile optimism
occasioned by a visit to a bookshop. Eitzel also brings an almost willful
"outsiderness" to his music and performances — on stage at a packed
Kilburn Luminaire he half-jokes, "I'm not like you!"

   We meet at the Soho landmark Maison Bertaux, and repair to a quieter
corner, chatting randomly *en route* about my new digital recorder, the UK's
"Underage" movement that in the past year or so has seen gigs and festivals
put on by teenagers for teenagers, and Eitzel's own first attempt-at-a-band —
a bunch of prog-rock inspired school friends in Southampton, UK, in the
mid-1970s who called themselves Instant Bucephalus (or maybe he was
winding me up). The band fell apart after five church hall rehearsals when
he discovered punk, reggae and Joan Armatrading.

IDLER: So how do you write? What's the
process?
MARK EITZEL: I wasn't kidding about
being endlessly lazy. I'll do everything
I can to avoid working, everything.
You know, endless, endless, *everything else
but* ... Except that I always have a note-
book, and I always make notes, and I'm
always trying to keep my mind focused
on a song. You know I'll play the song
before I leave the house and I'll play it
when I get home, because that keeps it
in your head. You kind of wait for those
moments when it all kind of sparks. You
can't rely on inspiration but with all
these notes you're kind of working out

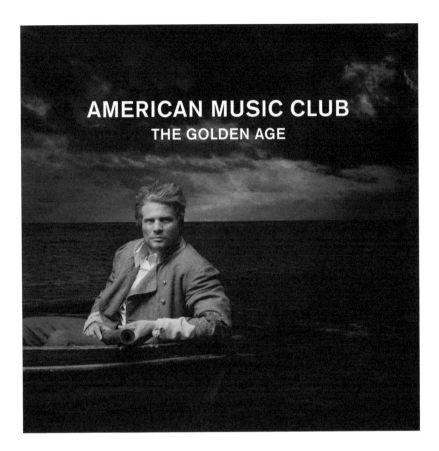

AMERICAN MUSIC CLUB
THE GOLDEN AGE

"what is it that this is?" And it kind of unfolds. You make it up too. Especially when you're a rhymer. I love that story about Charles Bukowski, who whenever he hated a poet he'd say [disdainfully], "Ah, that guy's just a rhymer." And I'm a rhymer!

IDLER: I always find it interesting how we all still continue to make work; to write songs, write books, against the balance of the odds. It's an Idler preoccupation—how to wrest your freedoms from The Man and try to sustain a creative life.

ME: Yes, ridiculously against the odds, sometimes. I think people grow older differently. There's no morality in it. Most of it's just habits and physiology. But also it's a philosophy that keeps you reading and keeps your mind not stultifying into ... Listen, testosterone is great, for fucking and making children and going and hunting and coming home, but it's also great for keeping you home and keeping you hunting and keeping you frozen in this isolated, incoherent male *dullness*, that I've noticed so many people just relax into. You know, great! It's not a bad thing. It's normal. But music really comes from enthusiasm.

IDLER: I read somewhere you said that a piece of music makes the world a better place.

ME: I really think so. Maybe there's too much of that. Maybe it's a desperate attempt to band-aid over the fall of the West or something. This is the last days of our golden era, it really is. It's amazing. There's so much good stuff happening now. I see bands that I just can't believe. I mean, talk about prog rock. I'll go to see some musician's amazing *side-project* and there'll be about twenty people there. And I just think, "as the empire falls; all this beautiful art."

IDLER: Which empire's collapsing? Are we talking climate change?

ME: No, just "the West". I'm sure that China will be a viscious, brutal empire, but it will be the next one. And the EU, if it survives, and it can't survive unless it learns how to deal with less oil. But I think America won't survive because it'll never be able to deal with any of those changes. You know, thirty years of spending more money on prisons than schools have left it kind of *over*. I'm talking about what so many Americans talk about, the theory of it, but it's the last remnant of the cold war; a failing cold war power with an increasingly despotic regime.

It's interesting. I was in Brighton last week, and I'm walking through the streets. Really not wanting to drink because there's so many people drinking and it was just like Saturday night and all these hen party girls with their matching outfits, stumbling around half-naked in the middle of the night, and drunk out of their minds. And everybody is out and I was, you know, it kind of frightens me a little bit. Not because it's threatening, but more because it makes me feel, "Oh, I've wasted so much of my life and they've wasted so much of their lives." But also, "I wish ... " because it's so beautiful and anarchic and crazy and great, and in that way frightening to me. And these cops were walking along, these bobbies, and they were smiling at the girls and the girls were being cheeky to them and it was all fun. There was no problem.

But in America everyone is so frightened of the cops. If the girls were being cheeky to [US] cops, they'd be on the ground, handcuffed, and thousands more cops would be called and suddenly it's a riot. Just because people were partying in the streets, having fun.

In New Orleans it could happen, it happens some of the time in San Fransisco. But where else in America? I don't know, New York, maybe. In the American government there's just instilled in everybody a fear of the people. A real fear! This leaking ship, trying to stay afloat with fear, and it really frightens me for America. Only twenty-four per-cent of Americans have a passport. They never leave. They never know that other people are freer than us. Other people are not afraid to speak, they're not afraid to ... I have a little thing on my website about how much I hate Bush. I did it myself. It's very amateurish, with links to MoveOn.org. It's kind of lame; middle-aged man style. But I'm kind of afraid of it now, because they're hiring a private corporation to track people who travel internationally and see what they say and do.

IDLER: Mapping dissent?

ME: Yes, and it's not government controlled. It's a private corporation that has to find results, you know. So you have this weird sort of power, this corporation that's feeding into government and completely bypassing any supposed rights that we're supposed to have, because it's a private corporation.

IDLER: So maybe in a couple of years they'll need to look for a new revenue stream, new kind of business model, and they've got all this data, so what are they going to do? Sell it, or look at ways to merge it with other databases, with RFID data?

ME: Exactly, so everywhere you go with your drivers licence and your RFID Chip — it's like driving down the freeway with a helicopter overhead, following you: "Oh yeah, you went there yesterday — you went to San Rafael, and you turned down the street, and we saw these other people that we suspect of being Al Qaeda were on the other side of the street ..."

IDLER: ... and you phoned them.' They just passed a law here — it was in the papers last year — that every telecoms company now has to keep a record of every phone call that's made — cell phones and everything. So that — the argument goes — during criminal investigations they can mine through this vast ocean of data. That's going to be a reality here.

ME: It'll be a reality everywhere. Visitors'

irises are scanned when they arrive in the US, but there's talk of this happening to everyone. And if you *don't* have your iris scanned, and you *don't* have an RFID chip, then you don't exist. Or you're a terrorist. And with the increasing divide between rich and poor in America, it's really frightening. But I hope I'll be dead before it all happens.

IDLER: But you know the expression it only takes two people to think the same thing and you have a conspiracy — and if the technology's there, it's going to be used. And like Naomi Klein's recent book, *The Shock Doctrine*; how the invasion of Iraq was parceled back to US corporations. It's already happening.

Bestselling author of *No Logo*

Naomi Klein

The Shock Doctrine

The Rise of Disaster Capitalism

ME: It's terrifying. They spent more in a month in Iraq than they've ever spent reconstructing New Orleans. The Spike Lee documentary, *When the Levees Broke*, was amazing — it really made you realise that there are two countries, that everyone in America lives on a knife edge between a bourgeois existence and the street.

IDLER: Like the title of that great cop novel by the San Fransisco writer Peter

Plate: *One Foot off the Gutter.*
ME: Yes, and there's nothing in between. Why do we pay taxes? Why have a government? Why call ourselves Americans?

IDLER: You're forced to collude. But in spite of that, here we all are making art. There's a great British writer, Rebecca West. She was writing about history and politics in Europe on the eve of World War II, and she says "art is a necessity... a cup into which life can be poured and lifted to the lips and tasted." But then she also goes on to say that in dangerous times — like these dangerous times — you've got to reach for it, because there's no other way to save yourself from becoming like them — the ones who inflict death and destruction on the rest of us. And then John Berger says the only way to counter Bush and co is to completely reject the terms of their discourse; to find the voices you want to join.
ME: Yes, I agree, but at the same time I don't trust artists that don't address that, that say, "I'm completely apolitical, completely uninterested in politics." Then I think, OK, then you're probably an ass-hole, you probably don't care about anyone else but yourself, you're probably a narcissistic fool.

IDLER: So do you go back to an idea like "the personal is political"?
ME: You know it's impossible for me to write anything [overtly] political — because in my private life I'm such a completely lost soul, and I can't really find a connection between my private life and the political — mostly because I hate political people so much. They always seem one step away from being fascists themselves, but then in America most people don't even know what the word "fascist" means! So you can't even use those words.

But OK, personal and political, the dot com boom: commercial spaces in San Fransisco went from being $2 a square foot to being $1600 a square foot, overnight. So all these artists, everyone from hippy candle-makers to recording studios were suddenly gone. I mean who cares really, things evolve, but it was a big part of what made San Fransisco interesting. This completely vibrant street culture. Not just white artists, all artists. People moved out.

A lot of the people that moved in were like these twenty year old kids getting six figure salaries for doing web design for these dotcoms. And they weren't nice. They were suburban kids that were used to the sense of entitlement. They really resented the street thing. They resented the lack of services: they couldn't park their fucking Mercedes! And they hated all the old guard artists. And these kids were not shy about saying, "Yeah, you had your time and, you know, we have a new revolution which is bringing this information highway." And I'm like "NO!

It's just a channel for fascism. You're middle-men, you're not *doing* anything, you're not *making* anything".

And this one kid said, "Well, what do you make?" So I said, "I make songs — I'm a songwriter." And he said, "Oh RIGHT! One of those! OK so you're a songwriter, what the fuck do you sell?" And I said, "Well I sell songs." And he said, "Oh yeah they're widgets, they're *just widgets* — think of it like that, that's all they are, wallpaper, something to sell." And I'm like, "Yeah, I get that, but there's something else, there's other kinds of value." And he's like, "No, there isn't!" So I asked him, "Have you ever read Rimbaud? Have you ever read *anything*?" And he said, "Who needs to read? I don't know who that is and I don't care!" And I ended up just picking up this bowl of fish crackers and said, "Yeah, here's your fucking *widgets*, here are *all of your souls!*" And I crushed 'em and I threw them in his face. It was not my best moment. I felt bad, but it's that weird thing of, I don't know, my personal and political don't always match up ...

PENGUIN CLASSICS

ARTHUR RIMBAUD
Selected Poems and Letters

IDLER: But there is actually some overtly political stuff on the last couple of albums. The kind of fascist parody on 'Homeland Pastoral', and the song 'Patriot's Heart', too.

ME: Well, you know, I'm a gay man and I was in Columbus Ohio a month or two after 9/11, and every other person had an American flag, or a bumper sticker, and you knew they probably didn't vote, you just have to look at the figures. So how patriotic is that? There's a right not to vote I guess, but if your're going to talk about patriotism then vote, support the system. You know I love America, but everyone should vote. Every republican, every democrat, every freak should vote. Change things. The way the system was set up it could have been this incredible thing, a very, very people-based voting system. But suddenly people going to the polls had to have two forms of ID, to prove they could vote. And if you went to a polling station that wasn't the one you registered at, you couldn't vote at all. So a lot of people didn't know, or if they showed up at the wrong polling station, or it moved and they didn't tell you, or you didn't read your mail, and you didn't have your passport and driving licence, then you're fucked. Millions of voters were disenfranchised.

So I was hanging out with this friend of mine and he said look we have to go to this one gay bar because the cops pulled everyone out and photgraphed them, so let's go! And it's a male strip club. So all these American flag cars are outside and inside, half of them are in the closet: all these older guys with sweaters and rugs and all their wives and kids at home! I just had the idea that the *real* Americans, the *real* patriots were the strippers, doing their thing on the edge and trying to be free. But don't start me off on the religion-will-destroy-the-world rant!

IDLER: It was the same in California, a flag on every lawn. But then, I was in New York right after 9/11 and it was different; more a kind of paralysing grief.

ME: Yes, and Susan Sontag said it best: "Let's by all means grieve together. But let's not be stupid together." Everyone in New York, all my friends, and I, were totally traumatised. But I have this friend, the poet Nicole Blackman who went down the World Trade Centre and said, "How can I help?" So they took her over to the Stuyvesant girls' school and the downstairs was going to be a place where they were going to feed all the firemen who were working in the pit, you know, Ground Zero. And it was just piles of boxes. There was no-one to organise this. So Nicole said, "Right! I'll do it!" And she was there for two months, 24-hours a day. The firemen started calling her "mama", and she's this diminutive young girl, not what the firemen would usually love, but it's New

York City where … God! What a great place! The best of America. It's such a great New York story: a Lower East Side art chick suddenly is this great hero. And it's so New York that they would let her.

IDLER: I'm not religious in any way, not at all, but I remember thinking, well, OK, George W Bush, *you're* supposedly a Christian, so what's the first thing you could have said? You know: "I Forgive them …"

ME: Yeah, "I forgive them. Now let's all do our best. Let's be the best we can be." How inspiring would that have been? But I was having a conversation with a British man, who loves America, and he said, "How come America's so diminished now?" And actually it starts right there, if our response to 9/11 is nothing but stupid-ass, dumb-ass revenge!

IDLER: But here we are hoping for something better …

ME: Well, yes, but the difference between us is that you have kids. You *have* to hope for something better. Me, I can just revel in my knowledge of the coming apocalypse. 🐌

See www.markeitzel.com and www.american-music-club.com for more information, including some great free downloads. Spike Lee, *When the Levees Broke: A Requiem in Four Acts*, 3 DVD set (HBO), £25.99
Peter Plate, *One Foot off the Gutter* (Seven Stories Press), £8.99
Naomi Klein, *The Shock Doctrine: The Rise of Disaster Capitalism* (Allen Lane), £25.00
Arthur Rimbaud, *Selected Poems and Letters* (Penguin Classics), £10.99
Rebecca West, *Black Lamb and Grey Falcon* (Canongate), £14.99
Nicole Blackman, *Blood Sugar* (Akashic Books), £9.99
'Harm's Way', Nicole Blackman's account of her 9/11 experiences at the Stuyvesant School is published by *La Petite Zine* at: http://www.lapetitezine.org/NicoleBlackman.htm & *New Yorker*, 24 September 2001: http://www.newyorker.com

BLOOD SUGAR
NICOLE BLACKMAN

"Sassy. Direct. Contemporary. Often merciless — impressive throughout." — GWENDOLYN BROOKS

THE ATTACK OF THE
LOSERS ON THE
WINNERS!

THIS TIME THERE'S MORE
OF THEM! THIS TIME
THEY CAN'T LOSE!

**WHATEVER YOU DO,
TAKE PRIDE.**

Games
DEFINITIALS
by Howard Male

¶ It felt like I'd fallen upon a magical secret of the English language when I discovered that you could define a word using the actual letters of the word as a starting point. What a thrill it was to find out, for example, that within the word ATOM was its perfectly succinct if unscientific definition: "A Titbit Of Matter". And is there a better way to sum up of the word DOGMA than "Deity Orders Grown Men Around"? Try it at home: wrtie down a few words and see who can come up with the best definitials.

STUFF Surprised Teddy Undergoes Forceful Filling

DRAGON Dangerous Reptilian Arsonist Gorges On Nubiles

MODEL Money-Obsessed. Diet Exclusively Lettuce?

KISS Kindness Is Sometimes Sensual

ELEPHANT Enormous Leaf Eating Pachyderm – Has A Nice Trunk

CENSORS Certain "Enlightened" Nobodies Snip Out Risqué Scenes

DRAMA Delights Really Awful Method Actors

DRAMA Doomed Romance As Murderer Advances

AIM Accuracy Is Maximized

CARROT Crunchy And Aromatic Rabbit Roughage. Orange, Tasty

COMET Cosmic Object Making Eternal Trip

DESCARTES Doubted Existence. Skeptical Catholic Argued Reason To
Establish Science

THE IDLER Tom Hodgkinson's Erudite Ideology: Do Little; Experience Rapture!

THE HUMAN TIME-BOMB!	HERE HE IS ON A BIT OF A DOWNER..	ANALYSING HIS TERRIFYING PREDICAMENT.

15 YeArs of IDLENESS

& the occasional publication . . .

1: August '93
SOLD OUT
Dr Johnson
Terence McKenna

2: Nov–Dec '93
SOLD OUT
Homer Simpson
Will Self

3: Jan–Feb '94
£8.00
Bertrand Russell
Charles Handy

4: April–May '94
SOLD OUT
Kurt Cobain
Matt Black

5: July–Aug '94
SOLD OUT
Douglas Coupland
Jerome K Jerome

6: Sept–Oct '94
SOLD OUT
Easy Listening
Richard Linklater

7: Dec–Jan '95
SOLD OUT
Sleep
Gilbert Shelton

8: Feb–Mar '95
SOLD OUT
Jeffrey Bernard
Robert Newman

9: May–June '95
SOLD OUT
Suzanne Moore
Positive Drinking

10: July–Aug '95
SOLD OUT
Damien Hirst
Will Self

11: Sept–Oct '95
£4.00
Keith Allen
Dole Life

12: Nov–Dec '95
£4.00
Bruce Robinson
All Night Garages

TO ORDER YOUR BACK ISSUES:

Go to www.idler.co.uk and order online
or make a cheque out to 'The Idler' and send it to:
The Idler, PO Box 280, Barnstaple, EX31 4QT, UK.
You must include P&P cost as follows:
Issues 1–24: 50p per issue. Issues 25–34: £2 per issue.
T-shirts £1 per item.
For European Community, add 50%. For Rest of the World, add 100%

40 BACK ISSUES

13: Jan–Feb '96
SOLD OUT
Stan Lee
Life As A Kid

14: Mar–Apr '96
£4.00
Bruce Reynolds
Will Self

15: May–Jun '96
SOLD OUT
Hashish Killers
Alex Chilton

16: Aug–Sept '96
SOLD OUT
John Michel
World Poker

17: Nov–Dec '96
SOLD OUT
John Cooper Clarke
Cary Grant

18: Spring '97
SOLD OUT
Thomas Pynchon
Ivan Illich

19: Summer '97
£4.00
Psychogeography
Henry Miller

20: Winter '97
SOLD OUT
Howard Marks
Kenny Kramer

21: Feb–March '98
SOLD OUT
The Gambler
Bez

22: April–May '98
SOLD OUT
Alan Moore
Alex James

23: June–July '98
SOLD OUT
Summer Special
Tim Roth

24: Aug–Sep '98
SOLD OUT
Krazy Golf
David Soul

MAN'S RUIN
25: Winter 1999
£15
The first book-format
Idler, featuring Louis
Theroux's Sick Notes,
Will Self, Howard Marks,
Adam and Joe
and Ken Kesey

PARADISE
26: Summer 2000
£5
Jonathan Coe
meets David Nobbs,
Nicholas Blincoe on
Sherlock Holmes, Tiki
Special, Iain Sinclair on
the London Eye

THE FOOL
27: Winter 2000
£5
Village Idiots,
Arthur Smith's diary,
The Big Quit, James Jarvis's
World Of Pain, John Lloyd

RETREAT
28: Summer 2001
£10
Louis Theroux
meets Bill Oddie,
Jonathan Ross meets Alan
Moore, Alex James meets
Patrick Moore, plus
Andrew Loog Oldham

HELL
29: Winter 2001
£10
Crass founder Penny
Rimbaud, Crap Jobs
Special, Boredom Section,
New fiction from Niall
Griffiths, Mark Manning,
Billy Childish

LOVE
30: Summer 2002
£10
Louis Theroux meets
Colin Wilson, Johnny Ball
on Descartes, Crap Towns,
Devon Retreat, Chris Yates
interview, Marchesa Casati

REVOLUTION
31: Winter 2002
£10
Dave Stewart, Black
Panthers, Saint Monday,
Allotments, Riots,
Introducing the Practical
Idler section

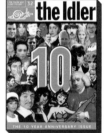

ANNIVERSARY
32: Winter 2003
£10
Damien Hirst on why
cunts sell shit to fools,
Marc Bolan, the pleasures
of the top deck, Walt
Whitman, happiness

To order go to
www.idler.co.uk

LADIES OF LEISURE
33: Spring 2004
£10
Clare Pollard is sick of shopping, Girls on bass, the wit and wisdom of Quentin Crisp; Barbara Ehrenreich

THE FOOD ISSUE
34: Winter 2004
£10
Joan Bakewell on life as a freelancer, Bill Drummond's soup adventure, The Giro Playboy, Falconry, why supermarkets are evil and Jerome K Jerome

WAR ON WORK
35: Spring 2005
£10
Keith Allen's A to Z of life, Raoul Vaneigem interview, Jeremy Deller's Folk Art, Dan Kieran's Seven Steps To The Idle Life, Chris Donald, Peter Doherty and more Crap Jobs

YOUR MONEY OR YOUR LIFE
36: Winter 2005
£10
Mutoid Waste Company, Edward Chancellor on credit, Penny Rimbaud, Jay Griffiths, A Hitch Hiker's Guide, the Guilds, Chris Donald

CHILDISH THINGS
37: Spring 2005
£10
Childcare for the Lazy, Michael Palin, Bertrand Russell, Free Range Education, Running Away to Join the Circus

THE GREEN MAN
38: Winter 2006
£10.99
Stephen Harding on why doing less is the way forward, Richard Benson tries to sow a meadow, in conversation with Jamie Reid, John Michell on Cobbett, plus ukulele special

LIE BACK & PROTEST
39: Spring 2007
£10.99
Penny Rimbaud on The Meaning of Life, Jay Griffiths eats missionaries for breakfast, Ronald Hutton, Green Gartside, LA Rowland explains why we shouldn't bother going to university

CARNAL KNOWLEDGE
40: Winter 2008
£10.99
Damien Hirst cover; Esther Perel on the sex drought, Neil Boorman, Nick Lezard, Michael Bywater, Sarah Janes and Kevin Godley

To order go to
www.idler.co.uk

A VIEW FROM THE SOFA

Greg Rowland gets inflated

¶ So I heard a lady from Zimbabwe talking about infla-
tion. She said that she bought her house five years ago. But, that very morning,
she had seen a banana on sale for the same price that she had paid for her house.
Not even a bunch, mind you, just one single banana. A bunch of bananas would
have got you a groovy condo in up-town Harare with a kidney-shaped swimming
pool, and flying robot-butlers. ¶ There's something morbidly fascinating about
hyperinflation. I always liked the probably apocryphal stories of Weimar Germany,
where you'd pay for a meal in a restaurant before you ate it because the price was
likely to go up in the course of fifteen minutes. Of course this assumed that somewhere in the back of each German café there was some guy with a ticker tape
machine reading out the prices on commodities like milk, tea, Toblerones and
mittnob-shlafflen and calculating precise expense hikes every quarter-hour. Of course,
in order to justify the time and expense of hiring such a person, the ticker tape
guy would probably bump up the prices a little further still, creating a further
inflationary spiral. ¶ Justifiably suspicious at this ruse, you might consider it
worthwhile to nip behind the counter and check if there was such a ticker-tape
tocker at work, but by the time you'd taken the necessary fifteen footsteps the
price of the your frankfurter would have rocketed exponentially, costing the
equivalent of a plumber's wages for 24 million years. Indeed, there is currently
a family in Düsseldorf who are still paying off the interest on their great-grand-
parents' injudicious order of extra *sauerkraut* in 1923, and are scheduled to
continue doing so even after our current solar system has gone into super-nova,
some five billion years hence. ¶ Perhaps, in the extended info-tsunami of the
electronic age, a similarly inflationary process has occurred. Has the Bodleian
Library become the banana of books? Has the internet become the wheelbarrow
of the wasteful currency of knowledge? Has the loping voodoo doll of the
episteme become pockmarked dismally by the ravages of that Google that you
do? Is knowledge not power, but poo? ¶ I have no answers to these pressing
questions. All I do know is that if you have too much of something then it ceases
to have value in the market. If the wisdom-wheelbarrow effect is to be avoided it's
important that we restrict ourselves to knowing no more than seventeen really
interesting facts, and just leave everything else well alone. ✆